Microsoft®

Windows® 7

Essential

Gary B. Shelly
Steven M. Freund
Raymond E. Enger

COURSE TECHNOLOGY
CENGAGE Learning™

Australia • Brazil • Japan • Korea • Mexico • Singapore • Spain • United Kingdom • United States

COURSE TECHNOLOGY
CENGAGE Learning™

Microsoft Windows 7
Essential
Gary B. Shelly
Steven M. Freund
Raymond E. Enger

Executive Editor: Kathleen McMahon

Product Manager: Klenda Martinez

Associate Product Manager: Jon Farnham

Editorial Assistant: Lauren Brody

Print Buyer: Julio Esperas

Director of Production: Patty Stephen

Content Project Manager: Matthew Hutchinson

Developmental Editor: Karen Stevens

Director of Marketing: Cheryl Costantini

Marketing Manager: Tristen Kendall

Marketing Coordinator: Stacey Leasca

QA Manuscript Reviewers: John Freitas,
    Danielle Shaw

Art Director: Marissa Falco

Cover Designer: Lisa Kuhn, Curio Press, LLC

Cover Photo: Tom Kates Photography

Compositor: Pre-Press PMG

Copyeditor: Karen Annett

Proofreader: Kathy Orrino

Indexer: Alexandra Nickerson

For product information and technology assistance, contact us at
Cengage Learning Customer & Sales Support, 1-800-354-9706

For permission to use material from this text or product, submit all requests online at **cengage.com/permissions**
Further permissions questions can be emailed to
permissionrequest@cengage.com

Library of Congress Control Number: 2009942961

ISBN-13: 978-1-4390-8107-5

ISBN-10: 1-4390-8107-7

Course Technology
20 Channel Center Street
Boston, MA 02210
USA

Cengage Learning is a leading provider of customized learning solutions with office locations around the globe, including Singapore, the United Kingdom, Australia, Mexico, Brazil, and Japan. Locate your local office at: **international.cengage.com/region**

Cengage Learning products are represented in Canada by Nelson Education, Ltd.

Visit our website **www.cengage.com/ct/shellycashman** to share and gain ideas on our textbooks!

To learn more about Course Technology, visit **www.cengage.com/coursetechnology**

Purchase any of our products at your local college store or at our preferred online store **www.CengageBrain.com**

Printed in the United States of America
1 2 3 4 5 6 16 15 14 13 12 11

Contents

Appendices

APPENDIX A
Comparison of the New Features of Windows 7 Editions

Preface

The Shelly Cashman Series® offers the finest textbooks in computer education. We are proud of the fact that our Microsoft Windows 3.1, Microsoft Windows 95, Microsoft Windows 98, Microsoft Windows 2000, Microsoft Windows XP, and Microsoft Windows Vista books have been so well received by students and instructors. With each new edition of our Windows books, we have made significant improvements based on the software and comments made by instructors and students.

Microsoft Windows contains many changes in the user interface and feature set. Recognizing that the new features and functionality of Microsoft Windows 7 would impact the way that students are taught skills, the Shelly Cashman Series development team carefully reviewed our pedagogy and analyzed its effectiveness in teaching today's student. An extensive customer survey produced results confirming what the series is best known for: its step-by-step, screen-by-screen instructions, its project-oriented approach, and the quality of its content.

We learned, though, that students entering computer courses today are different than students taking these classes just a few years ago. Students today read less, but need to retain more. They need not only to be able to perform skills, but to retain those skills and know how to apply them to different settings. Today's students need to be continually engaged and challenged to retain what they're learning.

As a result, we've renewed our commitment to focusing on the user and how they learn best. This commitment is reflected in every change we've made to our Windows 7 books.

Objectives of This Textbook

Microsoft Windows 7: Essential is intended for a course that includes an introduction to Windows 7. No experience with a computer is assumed, and no mathematics beyond the high school freshman level is required. The objectives of this book are:

- To teach the fundamentals of Microsoft Windows 7
- To expose students to practical examples of the computer as a useful tool
- To acquaint students with the proper procedures to manage and organize document storage options for coursework, professional purposes, and personal use
- To help students discover the underlying functionality of Windows 7 so they can become more productive
- To develop an exercise-oriented approach that allows learning by doing

Distinguishing Features

A Proven Pedagogy with an Emphasis on Project Planning Each chapter presents a practical problem to be solved, within a project planning framework. The project orientation is strengthened by the use of Plan Ahead boxes, that encourage critical thinking about how to proceed at various points in the project. Step-by-step instructions with supporting screens guide students through the steps. Instructional steps are supported by the Q&A, Experiment Step, and BTW features.

A Visually Engaging Book that Maintains Student Interest The step-by-step tasks, with supporting figures, provide a rich visual experience for the student. Call-outs on the screens that present both explanatory and navigational information provide students with information they need when they need to know it.

Supporting Reference Materials (Appendices) The appendices provide additional information about the Application at hand, such as the Help Feature and customizing the application.

Integration of the World Wide Web The World Wide Web is integrated into the Windows 7 learning experience by (1) BTW annotations; and (2) the Learn It Online section for each chapter.

End-of-Chapter Student Activities Extensive end of chapter activities provide a variety of reinforcement opportunities for students where they can apply and expand their skills through individual and group work.

Instructor Resources CD-ROM

The Instructor Resources include both teaching and testing aids.

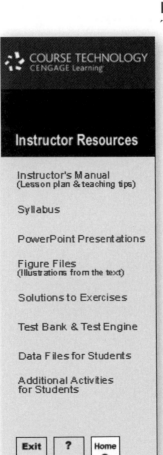

INSTRUCTOR'S MANUAL Includes lecture notes summarizing the chapter sections, figures and boxed elements found in every chapter, teacher tips, classroom activities, lab activities, and quick quizzes in Microsoft Word files.

SYLLABUS Easily customizable sample syllabi that cover policies, assignments, exams, and other course information.

FIGURE FILES Illustrations for every figure in the textbook in electronic form.

POWERPOINT PRESENTATIONS A multimedia lecture presentation system that provides slides for each chapter. Presentations are based on chapter objectives.

SOLUTIONS TO EXERCISES Includes solutions for all end-of-chapter and chapter reinforcement exercises.

TEST BANK & TEST ENGINE Test Banks include 112 questions for every chapter, featuring objective-based and critical thinking question types, and including page number references and figure references, when appropriate. Also included is the test engine, ExamView, the ultimate tool for your objective-based testing needs.

DATA FILES FOR STUDENTS Includes all the files that are required by students to complete the exercises.

ADDITIONAL ACTIVITIES FOR STUDENTS Consists of Chapter Reinforcement Exercises, which are true/false, multiple-choice, and short answer questions that help students gain confidence in the material learned.

Content for Online Learning

Course Technology has partnered with Blackboard, the leading distance learning solution provider and class-management platform today. The resources available for download with this title are the test banks in Blackboard- and WebCT-compatible formats. To access this material, simply visit our password-protected instructor resources available at www.cengage.com/coursetechnology. For additional information or for an instructor username and password, please contact your sales representative.

Blackboard

Guided Tours

Add excitement and interactivity to your classroom with "*A Guided Tour*" product line. Play one of the brief mini-movies to spice up your lecture and spark classroom discussion. Or, assign a movie for homework and ask students to complete the correlated assignment that accompanies each topic. "*A Guided Tour*" product line takes the prep-work out of providing your students with information on new technologies and software applications and helps keep students engaged with content relevant to their lives, all in under an hour!

CourseNotes

Course Technology's CourseNotes are six-panel quick reference cards that reinforce the most important concepts and features of a software application in a visual and user-friendly format. CourseNotes serve as a great reference tool during and after the student completes the course. CourseNotes are available for software applications, such as Microsoft Office 2007, Word 2007, PowerPoint 2007, Excel 2007, Access 2007, and Windows 7. There are also topic based CourseNotes available for Best Practices in Social Networking, Hot Topics in Technology, and Web 2.0. Visit www.cengage.com/ct/coursenotes to learn more!

SAM: Skills Assessment Manager

SAM is designed to help bring students from the classroom to the real world. It allows students to train and test on important computer skills in an active, hands-on environment.

SAM's easy-to-use system includes powerful interactive exams, training and projects on the most commonly used Microsoft® Office applications. SAM simulates the Office 2010 application environment, allowing students to demonstrate their knowledge and think through the skills by performing real-world tasks such as bolding word text or setting up slide transitions. Add in live-in-the-application projects and students are on their way to truly learning and applying skills to business-centric document.

Designed to be used with the Shelly Cashman Series, SAM includes handy page references, so students can print helpful study guides that match the Shelly Cashman Series textbooks used in class. For instructors, SAM also includes robust scheduling and reporting features.

Textbook Walk-Through

The Shelly Cashman Series Pedagogy:
Project-based — Step-by-Step — Variety of Assessments

Plan Ahead boxes prepare students to create successful projects by encouraging them to think strategically about what they are trying to accomplish before they begin working.

Step-by-step instructions now provide a context beyond the point-and-click. Each step provides information on why students are performing each task, or what will occur as a result.

Starting Windows 7

It is not an unusual occurrence for multiple people to use the same computer in a work, educational, recreational, or home setting. Windows 7 uses user accounts to organize the resources that are made available to a person when they use the computer. A **user account** identifies to Windows 7 which resources a person can use when using the computer. Associated with a user account is a **user name**, which identifies the person to Windows 7, and a **password**, a string of letters, numbers, and special characters, which is used to restrict access to a user account's resources to only those who know the password. In Windows 7, you can choose a picture to associate with your user name as well.

In a work or educational environment your user name and password might be assigned to you. Usually, you are given the option to reset the password to something that only you know. A good password is important for ensuring the security and privacy of your work. When you turn on the computer, an introductory screen consisting of the Windows logo and copyright message is displayed. The Windows logo is animated and glows as the Windows 7 operating system loads. After the Windows logo appears, if your computer is configured to start with **automatic logon**, your desktop will display on the screen without first asking you to type a user name or password. If your computer is not configured for automatic logon, the Welcome screen displays (Figure 4).

Determine a user name and password.
Before logging on to the computer, you must have a unique user name and password.

1. Choose a user name that is unique and inoffensive. Your user name may be provided to you in a work or educational setting.

2. Choose a password that no one can guess. Do not use any part of your first or last name, your spouse's or child's name, telephone number, street address, license plate number, or Social Security number.

3. Be sure your password is at least eight characters long, mixed with letters, numbers, and special characters.

4. Protect your password. Change your password frequently and do not disclose it to anyone or write it on a slip of paper kept near the computer. E-mail and telemarketing scams often ask you to disclose a password, so be wary, if you did not initiate the inquiry or telephone call.

Plan Ahead

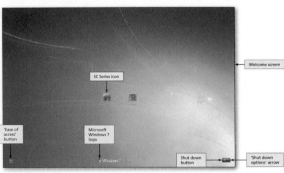

Figure 4

To Maximize and Restore a Window

Sometimes information shown in a window is not completely vi... tents in a window is to enlarge the window using the Maximize butt... window is filling the entire screen and you want to see part of the des... return the window to its previous state. The following steps maximize...

1

• Click the Maximize button on the title bar of the Computer window to maximize the Computer window (Figure 22).

Q&A When a window is maximized, can you also minimize it?
Yes. Click the Minimize button to minimize the window.

Figure 22

2

• Click the Restore Down button on the title bar of the Computer window to return the Computer window to its previous size (Figure 23).

Q&A What happens to the Restore Down button when I click it?
The Maximize button replaces the Restore Down button on the title bar.

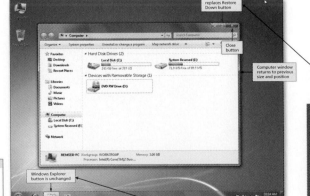

Figure 23

Other Ways

1. Right-click title bar, click Maximize, right-click title bar, click Restore
2. Double-click title bar, double-click title bar
3. Drag the title bar to top of screen; drag title bar to previous location

BTW

Screen Shots
Callouts in screenshots give students information they need, when they need to know it. The Series has always used plenty of callouts to ensure that students don't get lost. Now, use color to distinguish the content in the callouts to make them more meaningful.

Navigational callouts in red show students where to click.

Explanatory callouts summarize what is happening on screen.

Textbook Walk-Through

Q&A boxes offer questions students may have when working through the steps and provide additional information about what they are doing right where they need it.

Experiment Steps within our step-by-step instructions, encourage students to explore, experiment, and take advantage of the features of Windows 7. These steps are not necessary to complete the projects, but are designed to increase the confidence with the software and build problem-solving skills.

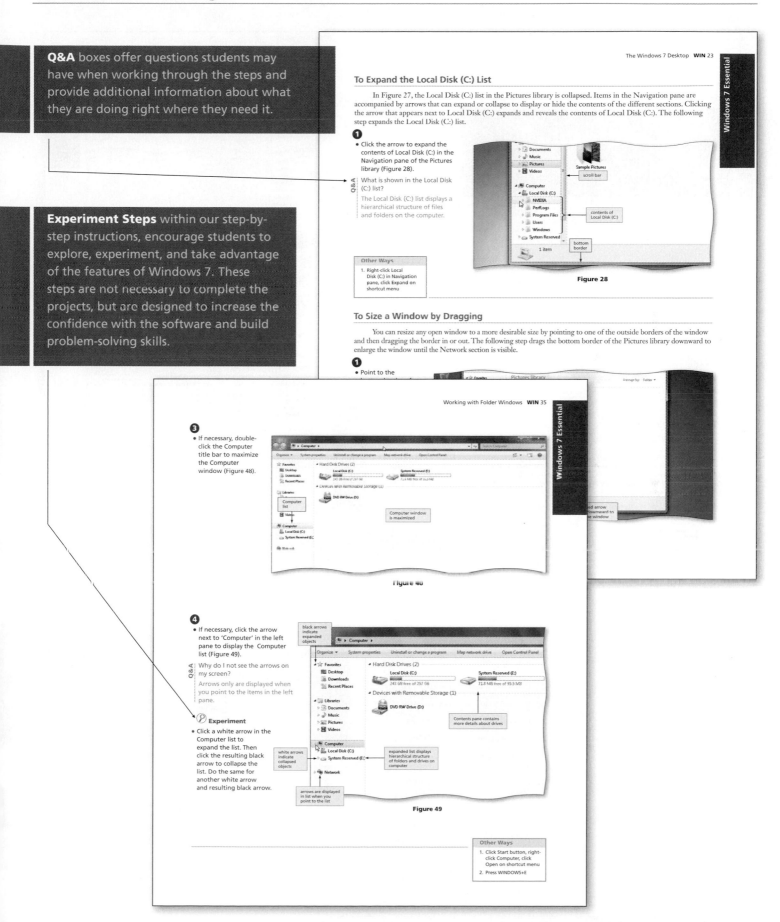

Windows 7 Essential

To Expand the Local Disk (C:) List

In Figure 27, the Local Disk (C:) list in the Pictures library is collapsed. Items in the Navigation pane are accompanied by arrows that can expand or collapse to display or hide the contents of the different sections. Clicking the arrow that appears next to Local Disk (C:) expands and reveals the contents of Local Disk (C:). The following step expands the Local Disk (C:) list.

1
- Click the arrow to expand the contents of Local Disk (C:) in the Navigation pane of the Pictures library (Figure 28).

What is shown in the Local Disk (C:) list?

The Local Disk (C:) list displays a hierarchical structure of files and folders on the computer.

Other Ways
1. Right-click Local Disk (C:) in Navigation pane, click Expand on shortcut menu

Figure 28

To Size a Window by Dragging

You can resize any open window to a more desirable size by pointing to one of the outside borders of the window and then dragging the border in or out. The following step drags the bottom border of the Pictures library downward to enlarge the window until the Network section is visible.

1
- Point to the

Windows 7 Essential

3
- If necessary, double-click the Computer title bar to maximize the Computer window (Figure 48).

Figure 48

4
- If necessary, click the arrow next to 'Computer' in the left pane to display the Computer list (Figure 49).

Why do I not see the arrows on my screen?

Arrows only are displayed when you point to the items in the left pane.

Experiment
- Click a white arrow in the Computer list to expand the list. Then click the resulting black arrow to collapse the list. Do the same for another white arrow and resulting black arrow.

Figure 49

Other Ways
1. Click Start button, right-click Computer, click Open on shortcut menu
2. Press WINDOWS+E

Textbook Walk-Through

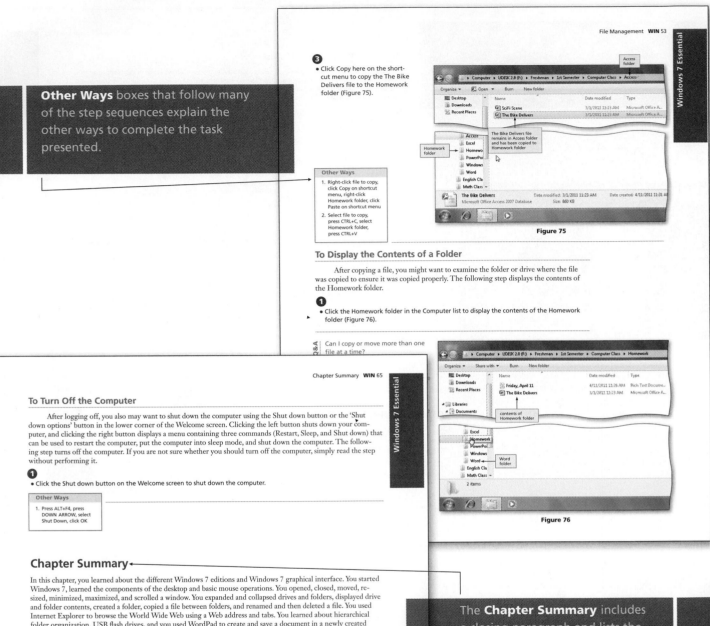

Other Ways boxes that follow many of the step sequences explain the other ways to complete the task presented.

❸
- Click Copy here on the short-cut menu to copy the The Bike Delivers file to the Homework folder (Figure 75).

Other Ways
1. Right-click file to copy, click Copy on shortcut menu, right-click Homework folder, click Paste on shortcut menu
2. Select file to copy, press CTRL+C, select Homework folder, press CTRL+V

Figure 75

To Display the Contents of a Folder

After copying a file, you might want to examine the folder or drive where the file was copied to ensure it was copied properly. The following step displays the contents of the Homework folder.

❶
- Click the Homework folder in the Computer list to display the contents of the Homework folder (Figure 76).

Can I copy or move more than one file at a time?

To Turn Off the Computer

After logging off, you also may want to shut down the computer using the Shut down button or the 'Shut down options' button in the lower corner of the Welcome screen. Clicking the left button shuts down your computer, and clicking the right button displays a menu containing three commands (Restart, Sleep, and Shut down) that can be used to restart the computer, put the computer into sleep mode, and shut down the computer. The following step turns off the computer. If you are not sure whether you should turn off the computer, simply read the step without performing it.

❶
- Click the Shut down button on the Welcome screen to shut down the computer.

Other Ways
1. Press ALT+F4, press DOWN ARROW, select Shut Down, click OK

Figure 76

Chapter Summary

In this chapter, you learned about the different Windows 7 editions and Windows 7 graphical interface. You started Windows 7, learned the components of the desktop and basic mouse operations. You opened, closed, moved, re-sized, minimized, maximized, and scrolled a window. You expanded and collapsed drives and folders, displayed drive and folder contents, created a folder, copied a file between folders, and renamed and then deleted a file. You used Internet Explorer to browse the World Wide Web using a Web address and tabs. You learned about hierarchical folder organization, USB flash drives, and you used WordPad to create and save a document in a newly created folder. You searched for files by typing a word in the Search box, you obtained Help using Windows 7, and shut down Windows 7.

The **Chapter Summary** includes a closing paragraph and lists the tasks completed within a chapter with pages references on which the step-by-step, screen-by-screen explanations appear.

1. Log On the Computer (WIN 8)
2. Add a Gadget to the Desktop (WIN 10)
3. Remove a Gadget from the Desktop (WIN 12)
4. Display the Start Menu (WIN 13)
5. Scroll Using Scroll Arrows, the Scroll Bar, and the Scroll Box (WIN 15)
6. Add an Icon to the Desktop (WIN 16)
7. Open a Window Using a Desktop Icon (WIN 18)
8. Minimize and Redisplay a Window (WIN 19)
9. Maximize and Restore a Window (WIN 20)
10. Close a Window (WIN 21)
11. Open a Window Using the Start Menu (WIN 21)
12. Move a Window by Dragging (WIN 22)
13. Expand the Local Disk (C:) List (WIN 23)
14. Size a Window by Dragging (WIN 23)
15. Collapse the Local Disk (C:) List (WIN 24)
16. Delete a Desktop Icon by Right-Dragging (WIN 25)
17. Start a Program Using the Start Menu (WIN 27)
18. Browse the Web by Entering a Web Address (WIN 30)
19. Open a Link on a New Tab (WIN 31)
20. Switch between Tabs (WIN 33)
21. Close a Tab (WIN 33)
22. Display the Computer Window (WIN 34)
23. Create a Folder on a USB Flash Drive (WIN 38)
24. Download a Hierarchy of Folders into the Freshman Folder (WIN 39)
25. Expand a Drive and its content (WIN 41)
26. Collapse a Folder (WIN 42)
27. Display the Contents of a Folder (WIN 43)
28. Start WordPad Using the Search Box (WIN 44)
29. Type Text (WIN 46)
30. Save a WordPad Document in a New Folder (WIN 46)
31. Verify the Contents of a Folder (WIN 51)
32. Copy a File by Right-Dragging (WIN 51)
33. Rename a File (WIN 54)
34. Delete a File by Right-Clicking (WIN 55)
35. Close Expanded Folders (WIN 56)
36. Start Windows Help and Support (WIN 57)
37. Browse for Help Topics in Windows Basics (WIN 59)
38. Search for Help Topics Using the Table of Contents (WIN 61)
39. Log Off the Computer (WIN 63)
40. Turn Off the Computer (WIN 65)

Textbook Walk-Through

Learn It Online

Test your knowledge of chapter content and key terms.

Instructions: To complete the Learn It Online exercises, start your browser, click the Address bar, and then enter the Web address `scsite.com/win7/learn`. When the Windows Learn It Online page is displayed, click the link for the exercise you want to complete and then read the instructions.

Chapter Reinforcement TF, MC, and SA
A series of true/false, multiple choice, and short answer questions that test your knowledge of the chapter content.

Flash Cards
An interactive learning environment where you identify chapter key terms associated with displayed definitions.

Practice Test
A series of multiple choice questions that test your knowledge of chapter content and key terms.

Who Wants To Be a Computer Genius?
An interactive game that challenges your knowledge of chapter content in the style of a television quiz show.

Wheel of Terms
An interactive game that challenges your knowledge of chapter key terms in the style of the television show *Wheel of Fortune*.

Crossword Puzzle Challenge
A crossword puzzle that challenges your knowledge of key terms presented in the chapter.

In the Lab

Using the guidelines, concepts, and skills presented in this chapter, complete the following Labs.

Lab 1: Improving Your Mouse Skills with Windows Gadgets
Instructions: Perform the following steps to play a game using a gadget.
1. Open the Start menu and then open All Programs. Click Desktop Gadget Gallery. Double-click the [...] add it to the desktop. Close the Gadget Gallery window.
[...] icture button on the Picture Puzzle to see what the picture will look like once you [...] Figure 95).
[...] Puzzle game, by moving the puzzle tiles around by clicking on them when they are [...]t. Continue to rearrange the tiles until you have completed the picture (you can [...]t any time to determine if you are close to the solution). Record your time here:
[...] button on the gadget to remove the gadget from the desktop.

> **Learn It Online** features six exercises, which includes True/False, Multiple Choice, Short Answer, Flash Cards, Practice Test, and Learning Games.

In the Lab

Lab 3: Getting Help
Instructions: Use a computer to perform the following tasks.
Part 1: Using Windows Basics to Get Help
1. If necessary, start Windows 7 and then log on the computer.
2. Display the Start menu and then click Help and Support.
3. If necessary, maximize the Windows Help and Support window.
4. Click Learn about Windows Basics link in the 'Not sure where to start?' area.
5. Click the 'Turning off your computer properly' link. What are the three ways to turn off your computer?

6. Click the Back button in the upper-left corner of the Windows Help and Support window.
7. Click the 'Getting started with printing' link below the Programs, files, and folders' heading. List the three types of printers and the most common type of printer connections.

8. Click the Back button in the upper-left corner of the Windows Help and Support window.
9. If necessary, scroll to view the Getting help topic below the 'Help and support' heading. Click the Getting help link. List the different ways you can get help.

10. Click the Back button twice to return to the Windows Help and Support home page.

Part 2: Browsing Help topics to Get Help
1. Click the 'Browse Help topics' link in the 'Not sure where to start?' area.
2. Click the 'E-mail and other communications' link. Click the 'When to trust an e-mail message' link. List the questions that can help you decide whether you should trust an e-mail message or attachment.

3. Click Windows Contacts (address book) in the Categories list.
4. Click the 'Managing your contacts' in the Contents list.
5. List the different types of information that can be stored in a contact.

6. Click the Back button three times to return to the Contents page.
7. Click the Security and privacy link in the Contents list.
8. What is the Action Center?

> The in-depth **In the Lab** assignments require students to utilize the chapter concepts and techniques to solve problems on a computer.

Introduction to Windows 7

Objectives

You will have mastered the material in this chapter when you can:

- Start Windows 7, log on the computer, and identify the objects on the desktop

- Customize the Windows desktop with gadgets

- Perform basic mouse operations

- Display the Start menu and start a program

- Open, minimize, maximize, restore, move, size, scroll, and close a window

- Display drive and folder contents

- Create a folder in folder windows and WordPad

- Browse the Web using Windows Internet Explorer 8, a Web address, and tabbed browsing

- Download folders from scsite.com

- Copy, move, rename, and delete files

- Search for files by entering a word in the Search box

- Use Windows 7 Help and Support

- Log off the computer and turn it off

1 | Introduction to Windows 7

What Is an Operating System?

An **operating system** is the set of computer instructions, called a computer program, that controls the allocation of computer hardware such as memory, hard disks, printers, and optical disc drives, and provides the capability for you to communicate with the computer. The most popular and widely used operating systems is **Microsoft Windows**. **Microsoft Windows 7** is the newest version of Microsoft Windows. Windows 7 allows you to communicate with and control the computer.

Project Planning Guidelines

Working with an operating system requires a basic knowledge of how to start the operating system, log on and log off the computer, and identify the objects on the Windows 7 desktop. As a starting point, you must be familiar with the Start menu and its commands, and be able to start a program. You should be able to personalize the operating system to allow you to work more efficiently. You will want to know how to manipulate windows as well as create a folder, display folder contents, recognize a disk drive, and download information from the Internet. You should be able to copy, move, rename, delete, and search for files. If you encounter a problem, Windows Help and Support is available to answer any questions you may have.

Overview

As you read through this chapter, you will learn how to use the Windows 7 operating system by performing these general tasks:

- Start the Windows 7 operating system.
- Log on the computer.
- Perform basic mouse operations.
- Add and remove a gadget on the desktop.
- Display the Start menu and start a program.
- Add and delete icons on the desktop.
- Open, minimize, maximize, restore, move, size, scroll, and close a window.
- Display drive and folder contents.
- Create folders and download folders from the Internet.
- Copy, move, rename, delete, and search for files.
- Use Help and Support.
- Log off and turn off the computer.

What Is a User Interface?

A **user interface** is the combination of hardware and software that you use to communicate with and control the computer. Through the user interface, you are able to make selections on the computer, request information from the computer, and respond to messages displayed by the computer.

Hardware and software together form the user interface. Among the hardware devices associated with a user interface are the monitor, keyboard, and mouse (Figure 1). The **monitor** displays messages and provides information. You respond by entering data in the form of a command or other response using an input device such as a **keyboard** or **mouse**.

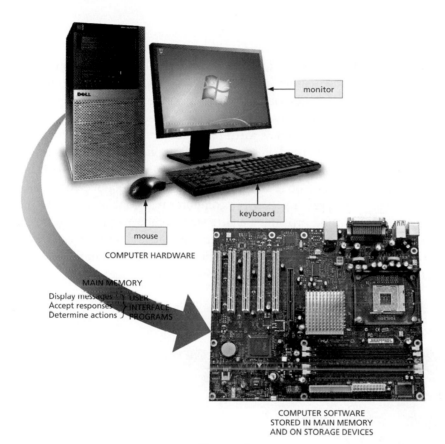

monitor

keyboard

mouse

COMPUTER HARDWARE

MAIN MEMORY

Display messages
Accept responses
Determine actions

USER
INTERFACE
PROGRAMS

COMPUTER SOFTWARE
STORED IN MAIN MEMORY
AND ON STORAGE DEVICES

Figure 1

The computer software associated with the user interface consists of the programs that allow you to communicate with the computer. The computer software determines the messages you receive, the manner in which you should respond, and the actions that occur based on your responses.

The goal of an effective user interface is to be **user-friendly**, which means the software can be used easily by individuals with limited training. A **graphical user interface**, or **GUI** (pronounced gooey), is a user interface that displays graphics in addition to text when it communicates with the user.

To communicate with the operating system, you can use a pointing device. A pointing device, such as a mouse or touch-sensitive pad, that may be built into the computer, attached to the computer with a cable, or may be wireless.

Many common tasks, such as logging on the computer or logging off, are performed by pointing to an item and then clicking the item. **Point** means you move the mouse across a flat surface until the mouse pointer on the monitor rests on the item of choice. As you move the mouse across a flat surface, the optical sensor on the underside of the mouse senses the movement of the mouse, and the mouse pointer moves across the computer desktop in the same direction. **Click** means you press and release the primary mouse button. The primary mouse button is the left mouse button. The right mouse button typically is the secondary mouse button. **Right-clicking** refers to the process of clicking the right, or secondary, mouse button. In most cases, you must point to an item before you click it.

Windows 7

The Windows 7 operating system simplifies the process of working with documents and programs by organizing the manner in which you interact with the computer, and using the computer to access information on the Internet. Windows 7 is used to run **application software** which consists of programs designed to make users more productive and/or assist them with personal tasks, such as word processing.

Windows 7 is commonly used on stand-alone computers, client computers, and mobile computers. A stand-alone computer is not part of a computer network, has access only to software that is installed on it and its hardware directly connected to it. A **client** is a computer connected to a server. A **server** is a computer that controls access to the hardware and software on a network and provides a centralized storage area for programs, data, and information. Notebook computers, including netbooks and Tablet PCs, can be used either as stand-alone computers or clients. Figure 2 illustrates a simple computer network consisting of a server, three client computers, and a laser printer connected to the server.

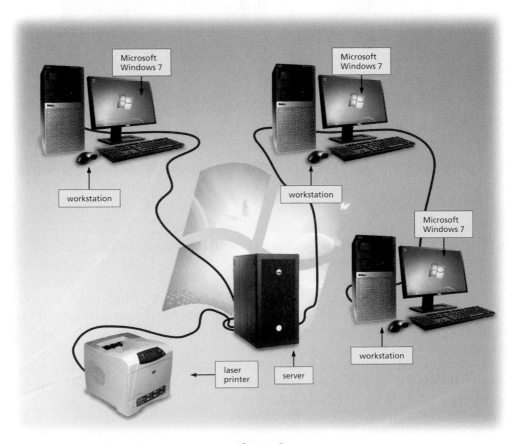

Figure 2

Windows 7 Operating System Editions

The Windows 7 operating system is available in a variety of editions. The editions that you most likely will encounter are Windows 7 Starter, Windows 7 Home Basic, Windows 7 Home Premium, Windows 7 Professional, Windows 7 Enterprise, and Windows 7 Ultimate. Because not all computers are the same, or used for similar functions, Microsoft offers these various editions so that each user can have the edition that best meets their needs. **Windows 7 Ultimate** is the most complete of all editions and includes all the power, security, mobility, and entertainment features. **Windows 7 Home Premium** contains many of the same features as Microsoft Windows 7 Ultimate, but is designed for entertainment and home use. The Home Premium edition allows you to establish a network of computers in the home that share a single Internet connection, share a device such as a printer or scanner, share files and folders, and play multicomputer games. You can create a home network using Ethernet cable, telephone wire, or wireless technologies. The six editions are briefly described in Table 1.

Table 1 Windows 7 Editions

Edition	Description
Windows 7 Starter	This edition contains the least number of features and mostly is used for computers with limited capabilities. Windows 7 Starter typically is installed by computer manufacturers and is generally not available in retail outlets.
Windows 7 Home Basic	This edition is designed for use in emerging markets only and lacks several new features. Similar to the Starter edition, Windows 7 Home Basic is installed by computer manufacturers and generally is not available in retail outlets.
Windows 7 Home Premium	This edition is designed for home users and includes features such as Windows Media Center, Windows Aero, and touch screen controls. This edition is available in retail outlets and is installed on new computers.
Windows 7 Professional	This edition is designed for small business users. It includes network and productivity features, backup and restore capabilities, and the ability to join domains. This edition is available in retail outlets and on new computers.
Windows 7 Enterprise	This edition is designed for enterprise customers who plan to install Windows 7 enterprise-wide. This edition includes additional features such as support for Multilingual User Interface packages and BitLocker Drive Encryption.
Windows 7 Ultimate	This edition contains all Windows 7 features and is designed for home and small business users who want all the features Windows 7 offers. This edition is the most expensive of the six Windows 7 editions.

BTW

Aero Enhancements
The Windows 7 Aero experience has been improved from the Windows Vista version. It now is designed to be easier to customize and is considered faster and more efficient than before. For example, Aero now allows live preview to display a window preview at full-screen size, along with a thumbnail size.

Windows 7 Interface

Windows 7 has two user interfaces: Windows 7 Basic and Windows 7 Aero. The Basic interface appears in the Starter and Home Basic editions of Windows 7. The Aero interface appears in all other editions as the default user interface. Aero is not available in the Starter or Home Basic editions, or might be disabled in other editions if the computer hardware does not support it.

The **Aero** interface features translucent colors along with various animations. To use Aero, your computer must have a compatible video card and an edition of Windows 7 installed that supports Aero. The first thing you will notice about Aero is **Aero Glass**, which is a translucent glass effect around the borders of the windows that allows you to partially see the items behind the windows. **Aero Flip 3D**, another component of the Aero experience, makes switching between your programs as visual and tactile as flipping through papers on your desk. Aero provides a simple and entertaining interface for working with Windows 7.

(a) Basic experience

title bars are transparent, allowing you to see contents of background windows

live preview shows contents of minimized window when you point to the program button on the taskbar

(b) Aero experience

Figure 3

Starting Windows 7

It is not an unusual occurrence for multiple people to use the same computer in a work, educational, recreational, or home setting. Windows 7 uses user accounts to organize the resources that are made available to a person when they use the computer. A **user account** identifies to Windows 7 which resources a person can use when using the computer. Associated with a user account is a **user name**, which identifies the person to Windows 7, and a **password**, a string of letters, numbers, and special characters, which is used to restrict access to a user account's resources to only those who know the password. In Windows 7, you can choose a picture to associate with your user name as well.

In a work or educational environment your user name and password might be assigned to you. Usually, you are given the option to reset the password to something that only you know. A good password is important for ensuring the security and privacy of your work. When you turn on the computer, an introductory screen consisting of the Windows logo and copyright message is displayed. The Windows logo is animated and glows as the Windows 7 operating system loads. After the Windows logo appears, if your computer is configured to start with **automatic logon**, your desktop will display on the screen without first asking you to type a user name or password. If your computer is not configured for automatic logon, the Welcome screen displays (Figure 4).

Determine a user name and password.

Before logging on to the computer, you must have a unique user name and password.

1. Choose a user name that is unique and inoffensive. Your user name may be provided to you in a work or educational setting.

2. Choose a password that no one can guess. Do not use any part of your first or last name, your spouse's or child's name, telephone number, street address, license plate number, or Social Security number.

3. Be sure your password is at least eight characters long, mixed with letters, numbers, and special characters.

4. Protect your password. Change your password frequently and do not disclose it to anyone or write it on a slip of paper kept near the computer. E-mail and telemarketing scams often ask you to disclose a password, so be wary, if you did not initiate the inquiry or telephone call.

Plan Ahead

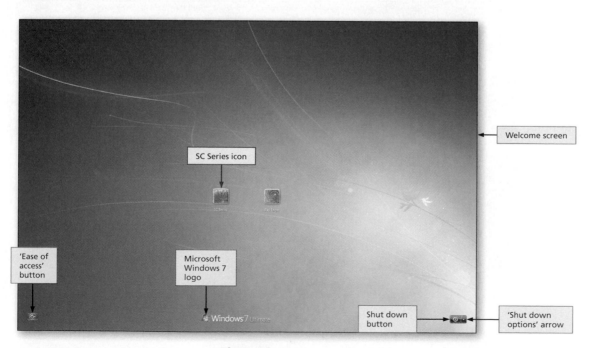

Figure 4

The Welcome screen shows the user names of every computer user on the computer. Clicking the user name or picture begins the process of logging on the computer. The list of user names on your computer will be different.

At the bottom of the Welcome screen is the 'Ease of access' button, Windows 7 logo, and a Shut down button. Clicking the 'Ease of access' button displays the Ease of Access Center. The Ease of Access Center provides access to tools you can use to optimize your computer to accomodate the needs of the mobility, hearing, and vision impaired. To the right of the 'Ease of access' button is the Windows 7 logo. Located in the lower corner of the Welcome screen is the Shut down button. Clicking this button shuts down the computer. To the right of the Shut down button is the 'Shut down options' arrow, which provides access to a menu containing the Restart, Sleep, Hibernate and Shut down commands.

The Restart command closes open programs, shuts down Windows 7, restarts Windows 7, and displays the Welcome screen. The Sleep command waits for Windows 7 to save your work and then turns off the fans and hard disk. To wake the computer from the Sleep state, press the Power button or lift the notebook computer cover, and log on the computer. The Hibernate command waits for Windows 7 to save your work and then turns off the computer. When you turn your computer back on after it has been Hibernating, you can start exactly from where you left off without waiting for the entire Windows 7 operating system to reload. The Shut down command shuts down the computer.

To Log On the Computer

After starting Windows 7, you must log on the computer. **Logging on** the computer opens your user account and makes the computer available for use. The following steps illustrate how to log on the computer. In this chapter, the user name SC Series is used in the figures.

- Click your user name on the Welcome screen to display the password text box.

Q&A | What is a text box?

A text box is a rectangular area in which you can enter text.

- Type your password in the password text box as shown in Figure 5.

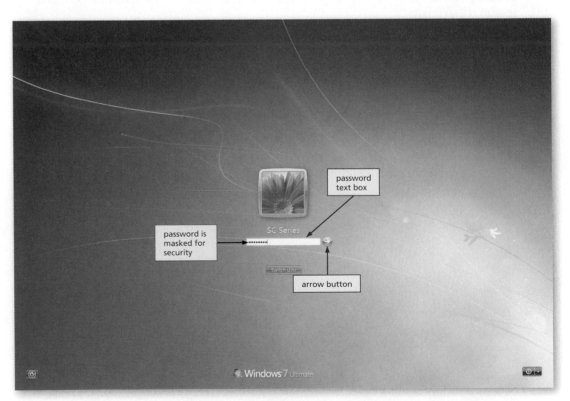

Figure 5

- Click the arrow button to log on the computer and display the Windows 7 desktop (Figure 6).

Q&A What is displayed on the desktop when I log on the computer?

The Recycle Bin icon and taskbar are displayed on the desktop.

Q&A What if the computer displays a different desktop design?

The Windows 7 desktop is customizable and your school or organization might have modified the desktop to meet its needs. For example, some schools customize their computer desktops with a picture of the school and/or the school name.

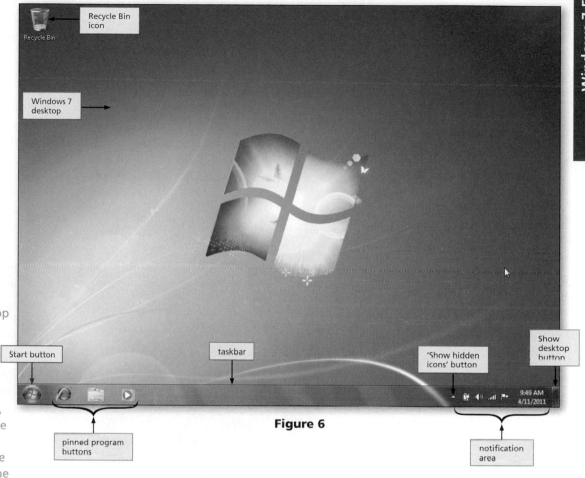

Figure 6

The Windows 7 Desktop

The Windows 7 desktop is similar to a real physical desktop. It is the main work area when you are using Windows 7. When you start a program, it appears on the desktop. Some items are on the desktop by default. For instance, the **Recycle Bin**, the location of files that have been deleted, is on the desktop by default. You can modify your desktop so that programs and files you use often are on your desktop and easily accessible.

The Windows 7 desktop can be customized to meet your needs. One way to customize the desktop is to add mini-programs called gadgets. A **gadget** is a mini-program that provides continuously updated information, such as current weather information, news updates, and online auction updates. In addition to the gadgets that come with Windows 7, you also can download additional gadgets online.

Across the bottom of the Windows 7 desktop is the taskbar (Figure 6). The taskbar contains the Start button, which you use to access programs, files, folders, and settings on your computer, taskbar button area, and notification area. The taskbar button area contains buttons that indicate which windows are open on the desktop. When a program has been **pinned** to the taskbar, a button with the program icon appears, regardless of whether the program is open or closed. By default, Internet Explorer, Windows Explorer, and Windows Media Player are pinned to the taskbar. **Windows Explorer** is a program that allows you to browse the files and folders on your computer. The notification area contains the notification icons, 'Show hidden icons' button, and the current time and date. The notification icons provide quick access to programs that are currently running in the background on your computer; that is, the programs are not displayed in plain view. The 'Show hidden icons' button indicates that there are one or more inactive notification icons.

To Add a Gadget to the Desktop

Gadgets can be added to the desktop according to personal preference. Gadgets can be found in the **Gadget Gallery**, which is a collection of gadgets. Before you can use gadgets, they must be added to the desktop. One method to add a gadget to the desktop is to double-click the gadget in the Gadget Gallery. **Double-click** means you quickly press and release the left mouse button twice without moving the mouse. The following steps open the Gadget Gallery and add a gadget to the desktop.

- Right-click the desktop to display a shortcut menu (Figure 7).

Q&A

What is a shortcut menu?

A shortcut menu appears when you right-click an object and includes commands specifically for use with the object clicked.

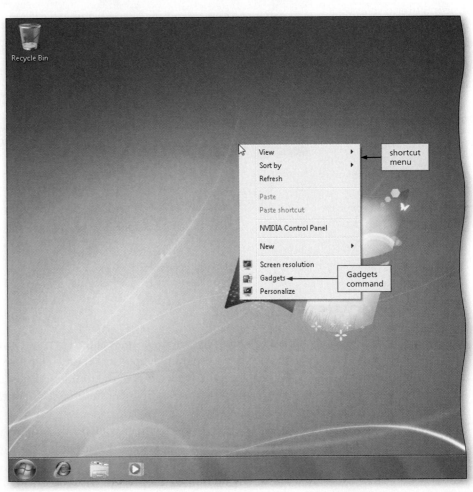

Figure 7

2

- Click Gadgets to open the Gadget Gallery on the desktop (Figure 8).

 Where can I find additional gadgets?

Click the 'Get more gadgets online' link to display the gadget collection on the Microsoft Web site.

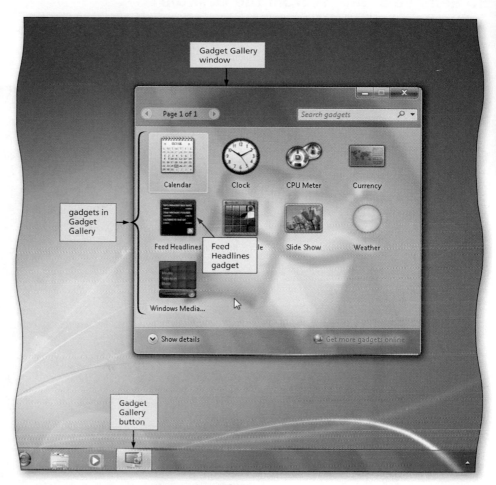

Figure 8

3

- Double-click the Feed Headlines gadget in the Gadget Gallery to add the gadget to the upper-right corner of the desktop and display frequently updated headlines (Figure 9).

4

- Click the Close button to close the Gadget Gallery.

 Can I customize the gadgets on the desktop?

Yes. You can select which gadgets you want to add or remove, add multiple instances of a particular gadget, and move them to any location on the desktop.

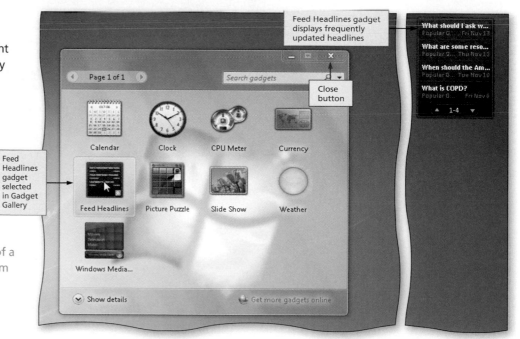

Figure 9

To Remove a Gadget from the Desktop

In addition to adding gadgets to the desktop, you might want to remove a gadget. The following steps illustrate how to remove a gadget from the desktop.

1
- Point to the Feed Headlines gadget to make the Close button visible (Figure 10).

2
- Click the Close button to remove the Feed Headlines gadget from the desktop.

Figure 10

Other Ways
1. Right-click gadget, click Close gadget

To Display the Start Menu

A **menu** is a list of related items, including folders, programs, and commands. Each **command** on a menu performs a specific action, such as searching for files or obtaining help. The **Start menu** allows you to access programs and files on the computer and contains commands that allow you to start programs, store and search for documents, customize the computer, and obtain help about thousands of topics. The Start menu contains the All Programs command, Search box, and left and right panes. The following steps display the Start menu, the All Programs list, and then the Accessories list.

- Click the Start button on the Windows 7 taskbar to display the Start menu (Figure 11).

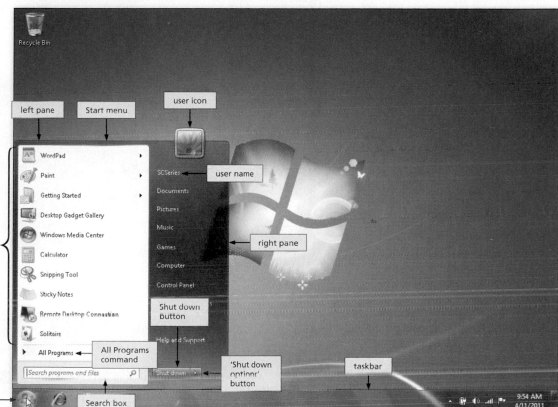

Figure 11

- Click All Programs at the bottom of the left pane on the Start menu to display the All Programs list (Figure 12).

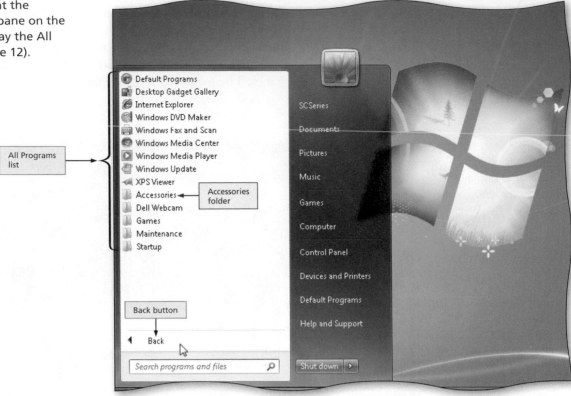

Figure 12

- Click Accessories to expand the list of programs and folders in the Accessories folder (Figure 13).

Q&A

What can I expect to find in the Accessories folder?

The Accessories folder contains programs that accomplish a variety of tasks commonly required on a computer. Most of these programs are installed with the Windows 7 operating system, such as Calculator, Snipping Tool, Windows Mobility Center (if you have a notebook computer), and WordPad. Your Accessories folder might contain additional or fewer programs.

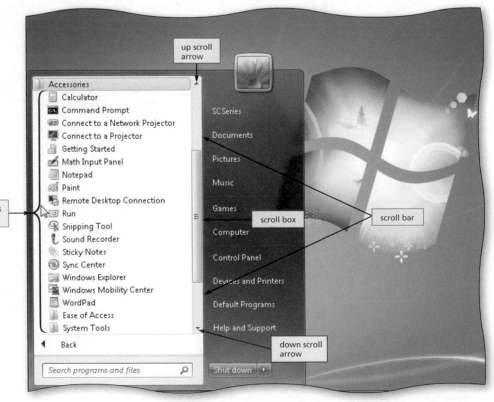

Figure 13

To Scroll Using Scroll Arrows, the Scroll Bar, and the Scroll Box

A scroll bar is a bar that displays when the contents of an area may not be completely visible. A vertical scroll bar, containing an up scroll arrow, a down scroll arrow, and a scroll box, enables you to view areas that currently are not visible. In Figure 14, a vertical scroll bar displays along the right side of the All Programs list. Scrolling can be accomplished in three ways: (1) click the scroll arrows; (2) click the scroll bar; and (3) drag the scroll box. **Drag** means you point to an item, hold down the left mouse button, move the item to the desired location, and then release the left mouse button. The following steps scroll the items in the All Programs list.

1

• Click the down scroll arrow on the vertical scroll bar to display additional folders at the bottom of the All Programs list (Figure 14). You may need to click more than once to show the bottom of the All Programs list.

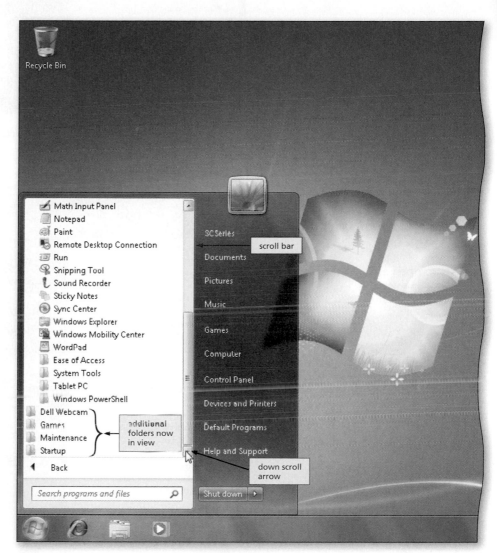

Figure 14

- Click the scroll bar above the scroll box to move the scroll box to the top of the scroll bar and display the top of the All Programs list (Figure 15).

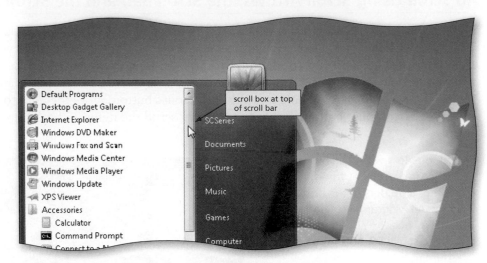

Figure 15

- Drag the scroll box down the scroll bar until the scroll box is about halfway down the scroll bar (Figure 16).

- Click an open area on the desktop to close the Start menu.

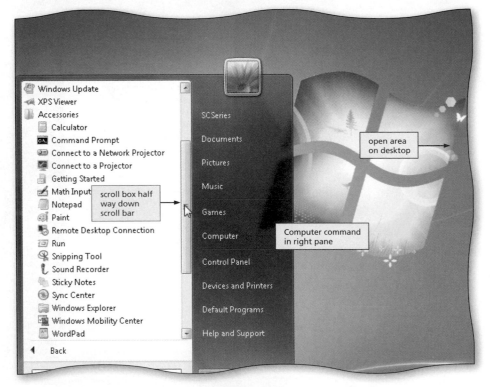

Figure 16

To Add an Icon to the Desktop

In addition to gadgets, you might want to add icons to the desktop. An **icon** is a picture that represents a file, folder, object, or program. For example, you could add the Computer icon to the desktop so that you can view the contents of the computer folder without having to use the Start menu. The following steps add the Computer icon to the desktop.

1

- Click the Start button to display the Start menu.

- Right-click Computer in the right pane to select the Computer link and display a shortcut menu (Figure 17).

Q&A Why should I use a shortcut menu?

A shortcut menu speeds up your work and adds flexibility to your interaction with the computer by making often used items available in multiple locations.

Figure 17

2

- Click Show on Desktop to close the shortcut menu and display the Computer icon on the desktop (Figure 18).

3

- Click an open area on the desktop to close the Start menu.

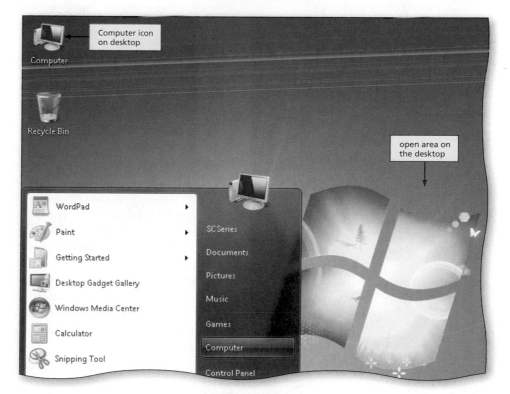

Figure 18

To Open a Window Using a Desktop Icon

When an icon is displayed on the desktop, you can use the icon to start the program or open the window it represents. One method for opening a window with a desktop icon is to double-click the icon. The following step opens the Computer window on the desktop by double-clicking the Computer icon on the desktop.

①

• Double-click the Computer icon on the desktop to open the Computer window (Figure 19).

Q&A

What does the Computer window allow me to do?

The Computer window allows you to view the contents of the computer.

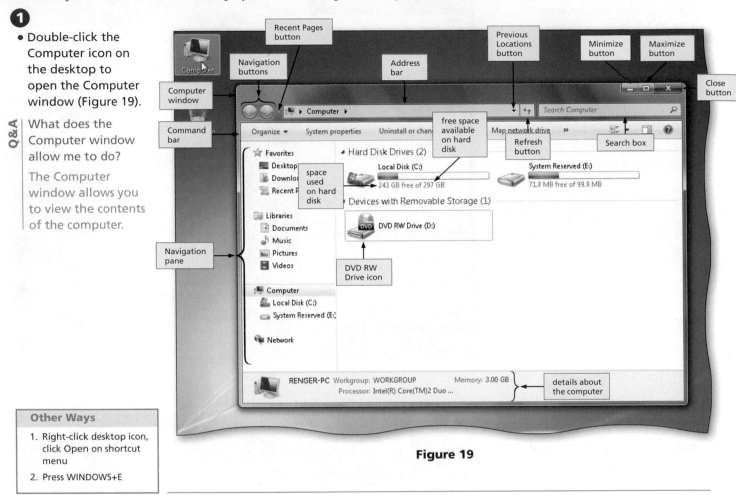

Figure 19

Other Ways

1. Right-click desktop icon, click Open on shortcut menu
2. Press WINDOWS+E

Folder Windows

Folder windows are the key tools for finding, viewing, and managing information on the computer. Folder windows have common design elements, illustrated in Figure 19. The three buttons to the left of the Address bar allow you to navigate through windows you recently have visited. On the right of the title bar are the Minimize button, Maximize button, and Close button that can be used to specify the size of the window or close the window.

The two right arrows on the Address bar allow you to visit different locations on the computer. The Previous Locations button displays a list of the locations you have visited using computer path names.

The Refresh button at the end of the Address bar loads the contents of the right pane of the Computer window. The Search box to the right of the Address bar contains the dimmed word, Search, followed by the location you are currently viewing. You can type a term in the Search box to search for files, folders, shortcuts, and programs containing that term within the specified location.

The Command bar contains five buttons used to accomplish various tasks on the computer related to organizing and managing the contents of the open window. The Navigation pane on the left contains the Favorites section, Libraries section, Computer section, and the Network section. The Favorites section contains links to your favorite locations. By default this list contains only links to your desktop, downloads and recent places. The Libraries section shows links to files and folders that have been included in a library.

A **library** is meant to help you manage multiple folders and files stored in various locations on your computer. It does not store the files and folders, but rather displays links to them so that you can access them quickly. For example, you can save pictures from your digital camera in any folder in any storage location on your computer. Normally, this would make management of the different folders difficult; however, if you add the folders to the Pictures library, you can access all your pictures no matter where they are stored on the hard disk.

Expanding the Computer section displays all of your folders in the classic folder list, or folder tree, that you may be familiar with from previous versions of Windows. Finally, the Network section lets you browse network locations.

To Minimize and Redisplay a Window

Two buttons on the title bar, the Minimize button and the Maximize button, allow you to control the way a window is displayed on the desktop. The following steps minimize and then redisplay the Computer window.

1

• Click the Minimize button on the title bar of the Computer window to minimize the Computer window (Figure 20).

Q&A

What happens to the Computer window when I click the Minimize button?

The Computer window still is available, but it no longer is the active window. It collapses to the Windows Explorer button on the taskbar.

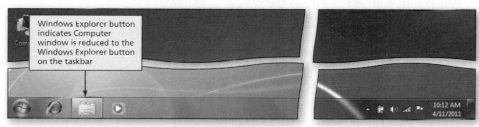

Windows Explorer button indicates Computer window is reduced to the Windows Explorer button on the taskbar

Figure 20

2

• Click the Windows Explorer button on the taskbar to display the Computer window (Figure 21).

Q&A

Why does the Windows Explorer button on the taskbar change?

The button changes to reflect the status of the Computer window. A lighter button indicates that the Computer window is active on the screen. A darker button indicates that the Computer window is not active, but is open.

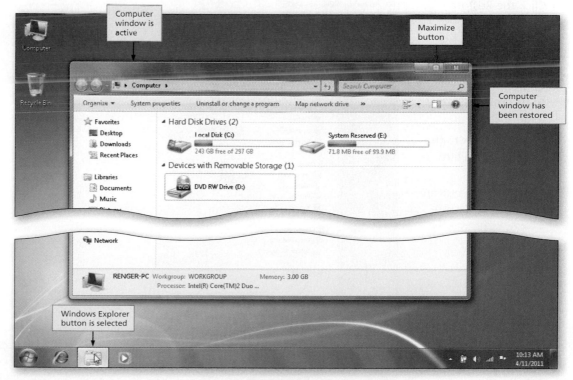

Figure 21

Other Ways	
1. Right-click title bar, click Minimize, on taskbar click taskbar button	2. Press WINDOWS+M, press WINDOWS+SHIFT+M

To Maximize and Restore a Window

Sometimes information shown in a window is not completely visible. One method of displaying more contents in a window is to enlarge the window using the Maximize button, so that the window fills the entire screen. If a window is filling the entire screen and you want to see part of the desktop, you can use the Restore Down button to return the window to its previous state. The following steps maximize and restore the Computer window.

1

• Click the Maximize button on the title bar of the Computer window to maximize the Computer window (Figure 22).

Q&A When a window is maximized, can you also minimize it?

Yes. Click the Minimize button to minimize the window.

Figure 22

2

• Click the Restore Down button on the title bar of the Computer window to return the Computer window to its previous size (Figure 23).

Q&A What happens to the Restore Down button when I click it?

The Maximize button replaces the Restore Down button on the title bar.

Other Ways

1. Right-click title bar, click Maximize, right-click title bar, click Restore
2. Double-click title bar, double-click title bar
3. Drag the title bar to top of screen; drag title bar to previous location

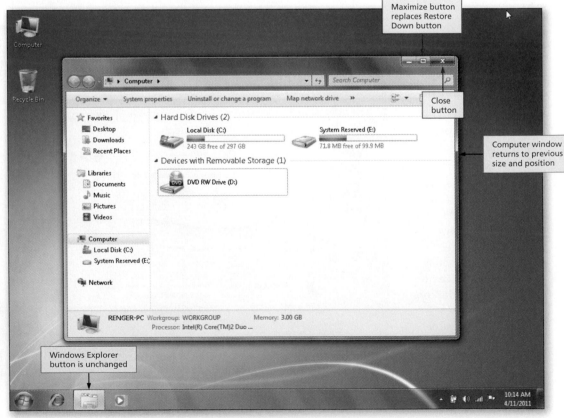

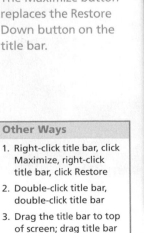

Figure 23

To Close a Window

You can click the Close button on the title bar of a window to close the window and remove the program button from the Windows taskbar. The following step closes the Computer window.

- Click the Close button on the title bar of the Computer window to close the Computer window (Figure 24).

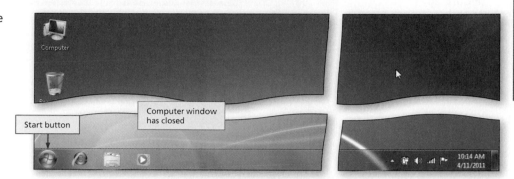

Figure 24

Other Ways
1. Right-click title bar,   2. Press ALT+F4
click Close

To Open a Window Using the Start Menu

Previously, you opened the Computer window by double-clicking the Computer icon on the desktop. Another method of opening a window and viewing the contents of the window is to use a command on the Start menu. The Pictures library is a convenient location to store your digital pictures, view and share your pictures, and edit pictures. The following steps open the Pictures library using the Pictures command on the Start menu.

- Click the Start button to display the Start menu (Figure 25).

Figure 25

● Click Pictures on the
Start menu to open
the Pictures library
(Figure 26).

Other Ways

1. Click Start button, right-
click Pictures, click Open

Figure 26

To Move a Window by Dragging

You can move any open window to another location on the desktop by pointing to the title bar of the window
and then dragging the window. The following step drags the Pictures library to the top of the desktop.

● Drag the Pictures
library title bar so
that the window
moves to the top
of the desktop as
shown in Figure 27.

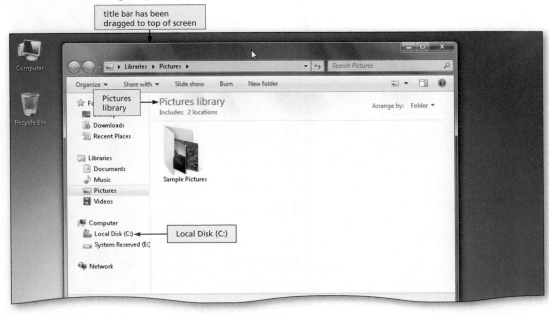

Other Ways

1. Right-click title bar, click
Move, drag window

Figure 27

To Expand the Local Disk (C:) List

In Figure 27, the Local Disk (C:) list in the Pictures library is collapsed. Items in the Navigation pane are accompanied by arrows that can expand or collapse to display or hide the contents of the different sections. Clicking the arrow that appears next to Local Disk (C:) expands and reveals the contents of Local Disk (C:). The following step expands the Local Disk (C:) list.

- Click the arrow to expand the contents of Local Disk (C:) in the Navigation pane of the Pictures library (Figure 28).

Q&A What is shown in the Local Disk (C:) list?

The Local Disk (C:) list displays a hierarchical structure of files and folders on the computer.

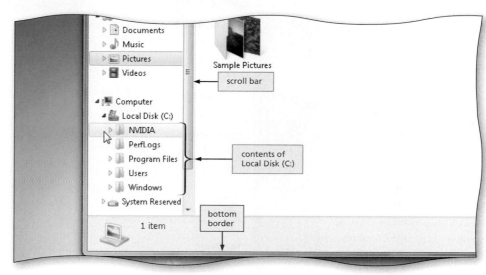

Figure 28

Other Ways

1. Right click Local Disk (C:) in Navigation pane, click Expand on shortcut menu

To Size a Window by Dragging

You can resize any open window to a more desirable size by pointing to one of the outside borders of the window and then dragging the border in or out. The following step drags the bottom border of the Pictures library downward to enlarge the window until the Network section is visible.

- Point to the bottom border of the Pictures library until the mouse pointer changes to a two-headed arrow.

- Drag the bottom border downward until the Network section is visible and the scroll bar no longer appears (Figure 29).

Q&A Can I drag the other borders to enlarge or shrink the window?

You can drag the left, right, and top borders and any window corner.

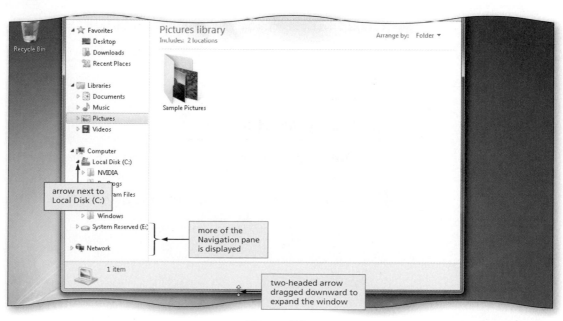

Figure 29

To Collapse the Local Disk (C:) List

When the Local Disk (C:) list is expanded, an arrow is displayed that points down and to the right. The following step collapses the list by clicking the arrow.

- Click the arrow to collapse the Local Disk (C:) list (Figure 30).

Q&A Should I keep the Local Disk (C:) list expanded or collapsed?

If you need to use the contents within the Local Disk (C:) list, it is handy to keep the Local Disk (C:) list expanded. You can collapse the Local Disk (C:) list when the information is not needed.

Figure 30

Other Ways

1. Right-click Local Disk (C:) button, click Collapse on shortcut menu

---

To Close a Window

After you have completed work in a window, normally you will close the window. The following step closes the Pictures library.

1 Click the Close button on the title bar to close the Pictures library.

To Delete a Desktop Icon by Right-Dragging

Sometimes, you will want to remove an icon from the desktop. One method of deleting an icon from the desktop is to right-drag the icon to the Recycle Bin icon on the desktop. **Right-drag** means you point to an item, hold down the right mouse button, move the item to the desired location, and then release the right mouse button. When you right-drag an object, a shortcut menu is displayed. The shortcut menu contains commands specifically for use with the object being dragged. The following steps delete the Computer icon by right-dragging the icon to the Recycle Bin icon. A **dialog box** is displayed whenever Windows 7 needs to convey information to you or wants you to enter information or select among several options. The Confirm Delete dialog box appears in the following steps.

- Point to the Computer icon on the desktop, hold down the right mouse button, drag the Computer icon over the Recycle Bin icon, and then release the right mouse button to display a shortcut menu (Figure 31).

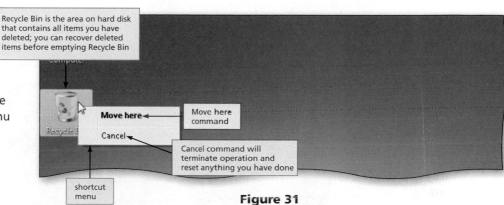

Figure 31

- Click Move here on the shortcut menu to close the shortcut menu and display the Confirm Delete dialog box (Figure 32).

Q&A

Why should I right-drag instead of simply dragging?

Although you can move icons by dragging with the primary (left) mouse button and by right-dragging with the secondary (right) mouse button, it is strongly suggested you right-drag because a shortcut menu appears and, in most cases, you can specify the exact operation you want to occur. When you drag using the left mouse button, a default operation takes place and that operation might not be the operation you intended to perform.

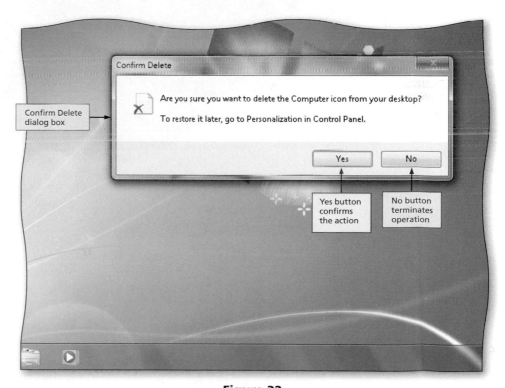

Figure 32

- Click the Yes button to delete the Computer icon and close the Confirm Delete dialog box.

Other Ways
1. Drag icon to Recycle Bin, click Yes button
2. Right-click icon, click Delete, click Yes button

The Keyboard and Keyboard Shortcuts

The **keyboard** is an input device on which you manually key in, or type, data. Figure 33 illustrates the rechargeable Natural Ergonomic Desktop 7000 keyboard designed for use with Microsoft programs and the Internet. Keyboards are basic input devices that provide USB ports for connecting hardware and offer specialized buttons which allow access to certain Windows 7 features at the touch of a button.

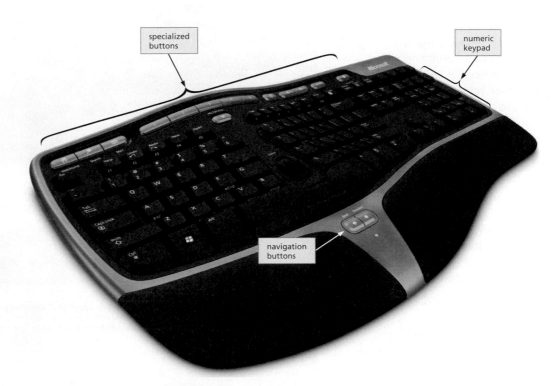

Figure 33

Many tasks you accomplish with a mouse also can be accomplished using a keyboard. To perform tasks using the keyboard, you must understand the notation used to identify which keys to press. This notation is used throughout this book to identify a **keyboard shortcut**.

Keyboard shortcuts consist of (1) pressing a single key (such as press the F1 key); or (2) pressing and holding down one key and pressing a second key, as shown by two key names separated by a plus sign (such as press CTRL+ESC). For example, to obtain help about Windows 7, you can press the F1 key, and to display the Start menu, hold down the CTRL key and then press the ESC key (press CRTL+ESC).

Starting a Program

One of the basic tasks you can perform using Windows 7 is starting a program. A **program** is a series of related instructions that tells a computer what tasks to perform and how to perform them. As previously mentioned, application software is a program designed to make users more productive and/or assist them with personal tasks. For example, a **word processing program** is application software that allows you to create and manipulate documents containing mostly text and sometimes graphics; a **presentation program** is application software that allows you to create visual aids for presentations to communicate with a group; and a **Web browser** is application software that allows you to access and view **Web pages**.

The default Web browser (Internet Explorer) appears as a pinned program on the taskbar shown in Figure 34. Windows **Internet Explorer**, also known as Internet Explorer, is a Web browser that allows you to perform tasks such as searching for and viewing Web pages, saving pages you find for use in the future, and maintaining a list of the Web pages you visit. Internet Explorer is included with the Windows 7 operating system or you can download it from the Internet. Because you easily can change the default Web browser on your computer, the default Web browser on your computer might be different. Another frequently used Web browser is **Mozilla Firefox**.

To Start a Program Using the Start Menu

A common activity performed on a computer is starting a program to accomplish specific tasks. You can start a program by using the Start menu. The following steps start Internet Explorer using the Internet Explorer command on the Start menu.

1
- Display the Start menu.
- Click All Programs to display the All Programs list (Figure 34).

Q&A
Can I start Internet Explorer by using the icon on the taskbar?

Yes. If Internet Explorer is not already open, you can click the icon that is pinned to the taskbar to start Internet Explorer.

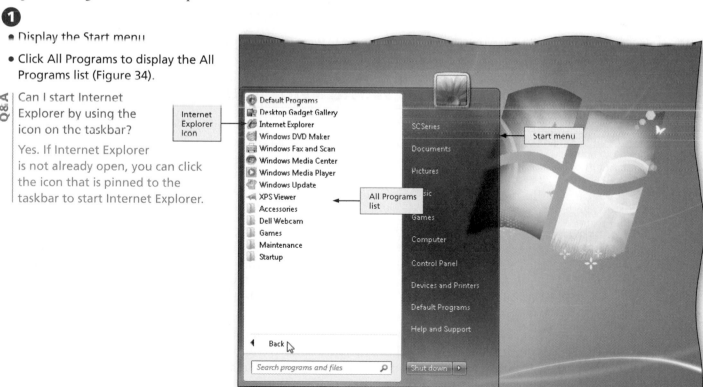

Figure 34

2

- Click Internet Explorer in the All Programs list on the Start menu to start Internet Explorer (Figure 35).

Q&A

What is displayed in the Internet Explorer window?

A title bar, Address bar, toolbar, Favorites bar, Command bar, Search box, scroll bar, status bar, and display area where Web pages are displayed.

Figure 35

Other Ways

1. Click Internet Explorer icon on taskbar

BTW

Web Sites
A collection of related Web pages on a computer is called a **Web site**. The MSN.com Web page shown in Figure 35 is the first Web page you see when you access the MSN.com Web site and is, therefore, referred to as a **home page**, or **start page**.

Browsing the World Wide Web

One method to browse the World Wide Web is to identify Web addresses of interesting Web sites in magazines or newspapers, on television, from friends, or even from just browsing the Web. Web addresses of well-known organizations usually contain the organization's name. For example, ibm.com is the Web address of the International Business Machines Corporation, and ucf.edu is the Web address for the University of Central Florida.

A **Web address**, sometimes called a Uniform Resource Locator (URL), is the address on the World Wide Web where a Web page is located. It often is composed of three parts (Figure 36). The first part is the protocol. A **protocol** is a set of rules. Most Web pages use the Hypertext Transfer Protocol. **Hypertext Transfer Protocol (HTTP)** describes the rules used to transmit Web pages electronically over the Internet. You enter the protocol in lowercase as http followed by a colon and two forward slashes (http://). If you do not begin a Web address with a protocol, Internet Explorer will assume it is http, and automatically will append http:// to the front of the Web address.

The second part of a Web address is the domain name. The **domain name** is the Internet address of the computer on the Internet where the Web page is located. The domain name in the Web address in Figure 36 is www.scsite.com. The last part of the domain name (com in Figure 36) indicates the type of organization that owns the Web site. Table 2 shows some types of organizations and their extensions. In addition to the domain name extensions listed in the table, there are country specific extensions, such as .uk for the United Kingdom and .dk for Denmark.

The optional third part of a Web address is the file specification of the Web page. The **file specification** includes the file name and possibly a directory or folder name. This information is called the **path**. If no file specification of a Web page is specified in the Web address, a default Web page is displayed.

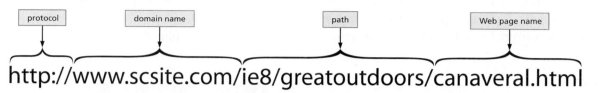

| protocol | domain name | path | Web page name |

http://www.scsite.com/ie8/greatoutdoors/canaveral.html

Figure 36

Table 2 Organizations and Their Domain Name Extensions	
Types of Organizations	**Original Domain Name Extensions**
Commercial organizations, businesses, and companies	.com
Educational institutions	.edu
Government agencies	.gov
Military organizations	.mil
Network providers	.net
Nonprofit organizations	.org
Types of Organizations	**Additional Domain Name Extensions**
Accredited museums	.museum
Aviation community members	.aero
Business cooperatives such as credit unions and rural electric co-ops	.coop
Businesses of all sizes	.biz
Businesses, organizations, or individuals providing general information	.info
Certified professionals such as doctors, lawyers, and accountants	.pro
Individuals or families	.name
Web sites offering media and other broadband content	.tv

To Browse the Web by Entering a Web Address

When you find a Web address of a Web page you want to visit, enter the Web address into the Address bar. The following steps display the Shelly Cashman Series Web site, which contains student resources for use with Shelly Cashman Series textbooks. The Web address for the Shelly Cashman Series Web site is www.scsite.com. You are not required to provide the leading http:// protocol when initially typing the Web address in the Address bar. Internet Explorer will insert http:// and assume the www automatically, if you do not supply it.

- Click the Address bar to select the Web address in the Address bar (Figure 37).

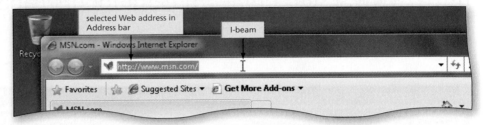

Figure 37

- Type
  www.scseries.com
  in the Address bar to
  enter the new Web
  address (Figure 38).

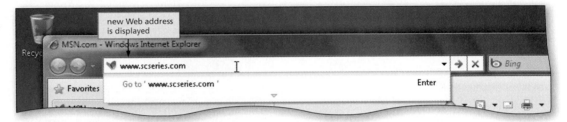

Figure 38

- Press the ENTER key to display the Shelly Cashman Series Web site (Figure 39).

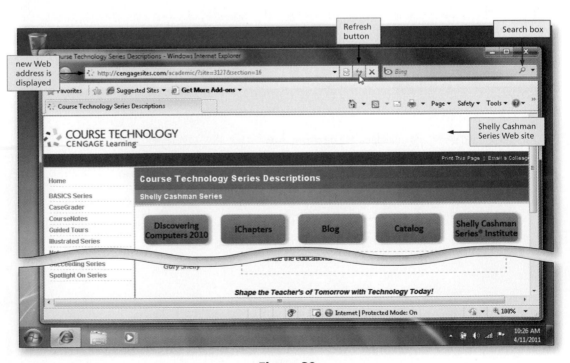

Figure 39

To Open a Link in a New Tab

You can view multiple Web pages in a single browser window using tabbed pages. A **tabbed page** consists of a tab in the Internet Explorer window and the associated Web page. When you start Internet Explorer only one tab is active, but you can open as many tabbed pages as you want. The following steps use the Search box and a link in the search results to open a new Web page on a new tabbed page.

- Click the Search box and then type Shelly Cashman Series (Figure 40).

Q&A

What is the Search box?

The Search box enables you to search the Web from the browser window. When you enter search text and then click the Search button, the selected search engine (in Figure 40 the search engine is Bing) will display your search results in the browser window.

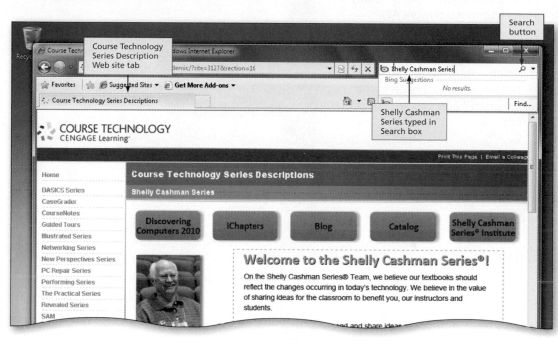

Figure 40

2

- Click the Search button to display the results of the Web search (Figure 41).

Figure 41

3

- If necessary, scroll to view the Course Technology Series Descriptions link.

- Right-click the Course Technology Series Descriptions link to display a shortcut menu (Figure 42).

Q&A

What happens when I just click a link?

The Web page will be displayed on the same tabbed page as the search results and will replace the search results page.

Figure 42

4

- Click Open in New Tab on the shortcut menu to close the shortcut menu and display the Course Technology Series Descriptions in a new tab (Figure 43).

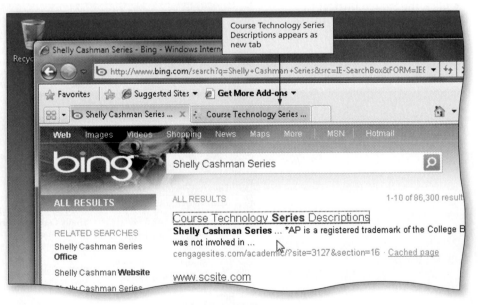

Figure 43

Other Ways

1. While holding down CTRL, click link

To Switch between Tabs

You can display the contents of any tabbed page by clicking the tab, as shown in the following step which activates the Course Technology Series Descriptions tab.

1

- If necessary, click the Course Technology Shelly Cashman Series tab to activate the tab and display The Shelly Cashman Series Web page in the display area (Figure 44).

Q&A

Why was the tab already displayed?

Depending on how your Web browser is configured, Internet Explorer might automatically display the contents of a new tab as soon as you open it. Otherwise, the tab might open in the background and you will have to click the tab to display its contents.

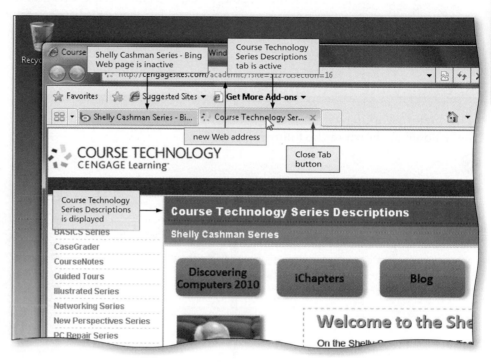

Figure 44

Other Ways

1. Press CTRL+TAB, press CTRL+TAB
2. Press CTRL+2, press CTRL+1

To Close a Tab

You can keep as many tabbed pages open as necessary. If you no longer have a need for the tabbed page to be open, you can close the tab using the following steps.

1

- Click the Close Tab button on the Course Technology Series Descriptions tab to close the tab (Figure 45).

2

- Click the Close button on the title bar to close Internet Explorer.

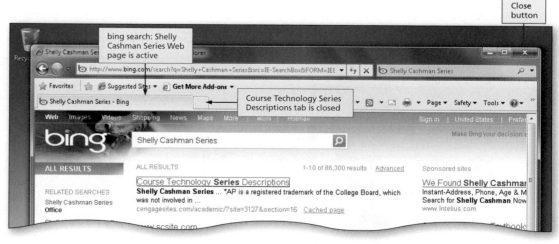

Figure 45

Working with Folder Windows

Folder windows in Windows 7 allow you to view the contents of the computer, the hierarchy of drives and folders on the computer, and the files and folders in each folder. In additon, you can expand and collapse drives and folders, display drive and folder contents, create a new folder, copy a file between folders, and rename and then delete a file. These common operations allow users to interact with the computer more efficiently.

To Display the Computer Window

Before working with folders, you must display the Start menu, open the Computer window, and then maximize the window, as shown in the following steps.

- Display the Start menu (Figure 46).

Figure 46

- Click Computer on the Start menu to open the Computer window (Figure 47).

Figure 47

3

• If necessary, double-click the Computer title bar to maximize the Computer window (Figure 48).

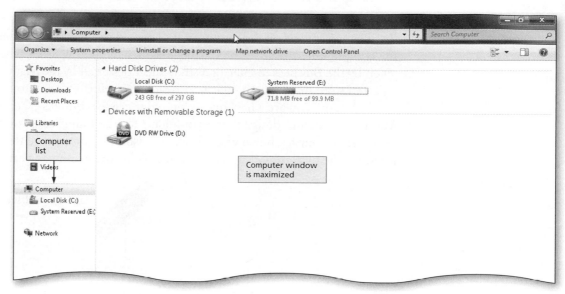

Figure 48

4

• If necessary, click the arrow next to 'Computer' in the left pane to display the Computer list (Figure 49).

 Q&A Why do I not see the arrows on my screen?

Arrows only are displayed when you point to the items in the left pane.

Experiment

• Click a white arrow in the Computer list to expand the list. Then click the resulting black arrow to collapse the list. Do the same for another white arrow and resulting black arrow.

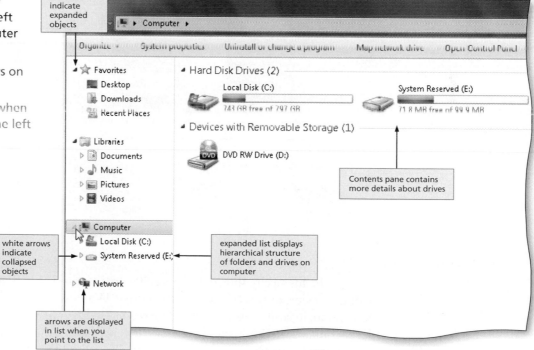

Figure 49

Other Ways
1. Click Start button, right-click Computer, click Open on shortcut menu
2. Press WINDOWS+E

Using a Hierarchical Format to Organize Files and Folders

In addition to navigating drives and folders, you also need to be able to create and organize the files and folders on the computer. A file could contain a spreadsheet assignment given by the computer teacher, a research paper assigned by the English teacher, an electronic quiz given by the Business teacher, or a study sheet designed by the Math teacher. You should organize and store these files in folders to avoid misplacing a file and to help you find a file quickly.

Assume you are a freshman taking four classes (Business, Computer, English, and Math). You want to design a series of folders for the four classes you are taking in the first semester of your freshman year. To accomplish this, you arrange the folders in a **hierarchical format**. The hierarchical structure of folders for the Freshman year is shown in Figure 50.

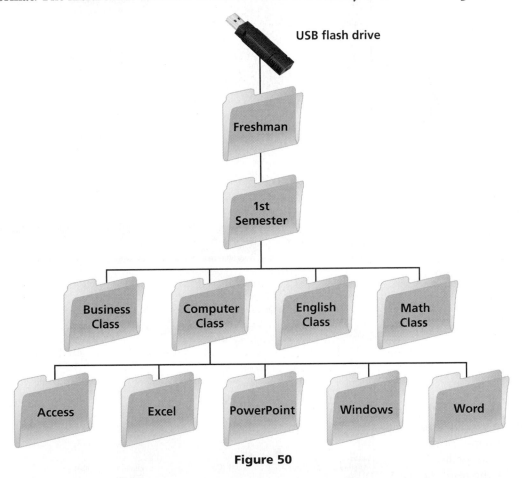

Figure 50

The hierarchy shown in Figure 50 contains five levels. The first level contains the storage device, in this case a USB flash drive. Windows 7 identifies the storage device with a letter, and, in some cases, a name. The second level contains the Freshman folder, the third level contains the 1st Semester folder, the fourth level contains four folders (Business Class, Computer Class, English Class, and Math Class), and the fifth level contains five folders (Access, Excel, PowerPoint, Windows, and Word).

The vertical and horizontal lines in the hierarchy chart form a pathway that allows you to navigate to a drive or folder. Each pathway is a means of navigation to a specific location on a computer or network. A **path** consists of a drive letter (preceded by a drive name when necessary) and colon, to identify the storage device, and one or more folder names. Each drive or folder in the hierarchy chart has a corresponding path. When you click a drive or folder icon in the Folders list, the corresponding path appears in the Address bar. Table 3 contains examples of paths and their corresponding drives and folders. These paths are referred to as **breadcrumb trails**, showing you where the current page or folder is in the hierarchy.

When the hierarchy in Figure 50 is created, the USB flash drive is said "to contain" the Freshman folder, the Freshman folder is said "to contain" the 1st Semester folder, and so on. In addition, this hierarchy can easily be expanded to include folders from the Sophomore, Junior, and Senior years and any additional semesters.

Table 3 Address Bar Location

Path	Drive and Folder
Computer ► UDISK 2.0 (F:)	Drive F (UDISK 2.0 (F:))
Computer ► UDISK 2.0 (F:) ► Freshman	Freshman folder on drive F
Computer ► UDISK 2.0 (F:) ► Freshman ► 1st Semester	1st Semester folder in Freshman folder on drive F
Computer ► UDISK 2.0 (F:) ► Freshman ► 1st Semester ► Computer Class ► Word	Word folder in Computer Class folder in 1st Semester folder in Freshman folder on drive F

Removable Media and Network Drives

Types of removable media such as USB flash drives are ideal for storing files and folders on a computer. A **USB flash drive**, sometimes called a thumb drive or jump drive, is a flash memory storage device that plugs in a USB port on a computer. A **USB port**, short for universal serial bus port, can be found on most computers. USB flash drives, like the one shown in Figure 51, are convenient for mobile users because they are small and light-weight enough to be transported on a keychain or in a pocket.

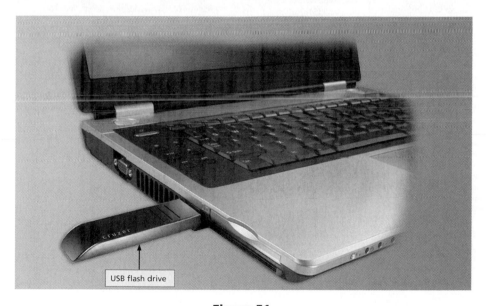

USB flash drive

Figure 51

Instead of a USB flash drive, you might use files stored on a network drive. A **network** is a collection of computers and devices connected together for the purpose of sharing resources. In some cases, students might be required to store their files on a network drive found on the school's computer network. A **network drive** is a storage device that is connected to the server on the computer network. A **server** controls access to the hardware, software, and other resources on the network and provides a centralized storage area for programs, data, and information. If student files reside on the network drive on the school's network, files may be accessed from a school computer, or from a personal computer with permission from the school.

To Create a Folder on a USB Flash Drive

When you create a folder, such as the Freshman folder in Figure 50 on page WIN 36, you must name the folder. A folder name should describe the folder and its contents. The following steps create the Freshman folder on the UDISK 2.0 (F:) drive.

1

- Connect a USB flash drive to an available USB port to display the AutoPlay dialog box (Figure 52).

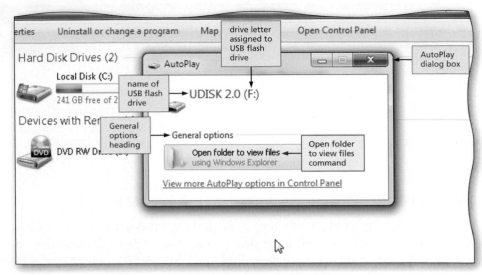

Figure 52

2

- Under the General options heading, click 'Open folder to view files' to open a folder window to display the contents of your USB flash drive (Figure 53).

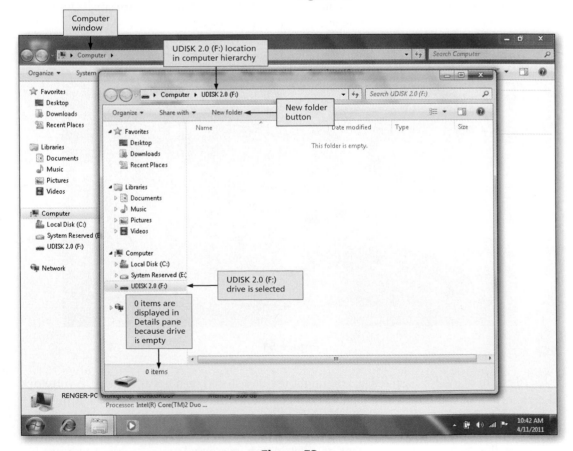

Figure 53

3
- Click New folder on the toolbar to display the New folder icon.

- Type Freshman in the text box to name the folder.

- Press the ENTER key to create the Freshman folder on the UDISK 2.0 (F:) drive (Figure 54).

Q&A What happens when I press the ENTER key?

The Freshman folder is displayed in the File list, which contains the folder name, date modified, type, and size.

Q&A Are there any restrictions when naming a folder?

A folder name can contain up to 255 characters, including spaces. Any uppercase or lowercase character is valid when creating a folder name, except a backslash (\), slash (/), colon (:), asterisk (*), question mark (?), quotation marks ("), less than symbol (<), greater than symbol (>), or vertical bar (|). Folder names cannot be CON, AUX, COM1, COM2, COM3, COM4, LPT1, LPT2, LPT3, PRN, or NUL. The same rules for naming folders also apply to naming files.

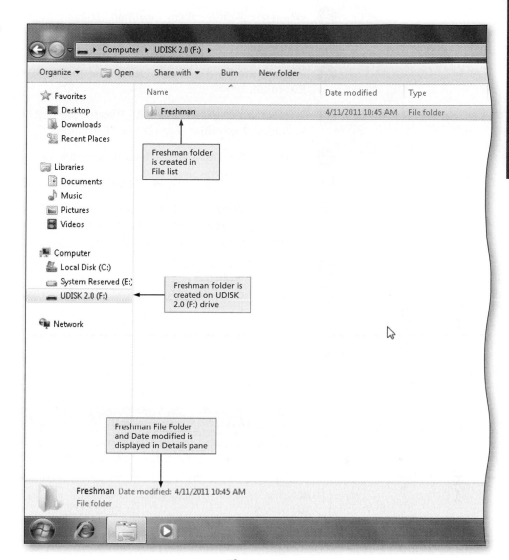

Figure 54

To Download a Hierarchy of Folders into the Freshman Folder

After creating the Freshman folder on the USB flash drive, the remaining folders in the hierarchical structure (see Figure 50 on page WIN 36), starting with the 1st Semester folder, should be downloaded to the Freshman folder. **Downloading** is the process of a computer receiving information, such as a set of files or folders from a Web site, from a server on the Internet. To make the task of creating the folders easier, the folders have been created and stored in a hierarchical structure on the Shelly Cashman Series Web site. The following steps download the folders in the hierarchical structure into the Freshman folder.

1 Start Internet Explorer by clicking the Internet Explorer icon on the taskbar.

2 Click the Address bar, type scsite.com in the Address bar, and then press the ENTER key.

3 When the SC Site - Shelly Cashman Series Student Resources Web page is displayed, use the Browse by Subject navigation bar, click Operating Systems, and then click Microsoft Windows.

4 In the center of the screen, locate your textbook and click the title (Microsoft Windows 7: Essential).

5 Scroll down to display the Data Files for Students (Windows) area and then click the Windows 7 Essential Chapter Data Files link.

6 When the File Download – Security Warning dialog box is displayed, click the Run button.

7 When the Internet Explorer – Security Warning dialog box is displayed, click the Run button.

8 When the WinZip Self-Extractor dialog box is displayed, type the removable media drive letter of your removable media drive followed by a colon, backslash, and folder name (Freshman) (for example, F:\Freshman).

9 Click the Unzip button.

10 When Windows displays the WinZip Self-Extractor dialog box, click the OK button.

11 Click the Close button in the WinZip Self-Extractor dialog box.

12 Close the Shelly Cashman Series Web site window (Figure 55).

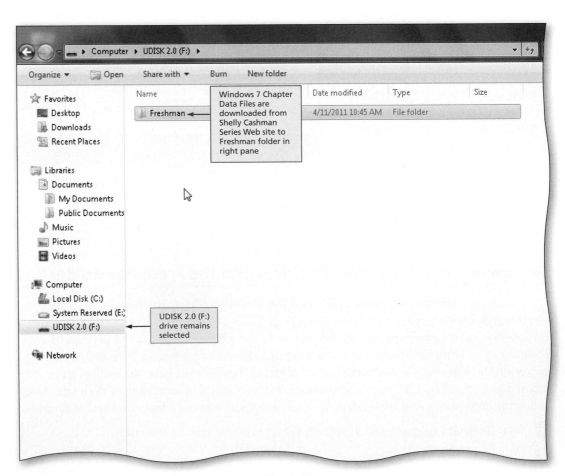

Figure 55

To Expand a Drive and Its Content

    Folder windows display the hierarchy of items in the Folders list and the contents of drives and folders in the right pane. You might want to expand a drive to view its contents in the Folders list. The following step expands a drive.

- Point to any item in the Folders list to display arrows, and then click the white arrow to the left of the UDISK 2.0 (F:) icon in the Folders list to display the Freshman folder.

Q&A

Why are black arrows and white arrows in the Folders list?

The black arrows represent folders and drives that contain other folders that have been expanded to show their contents. The white arrows represent folders and drives that contain other folders that have not been expanded.

- Click the white arrow next to the Freshman folder, and then click the white arrow next to the 1st Semester folder to display its contents (Figure 56).

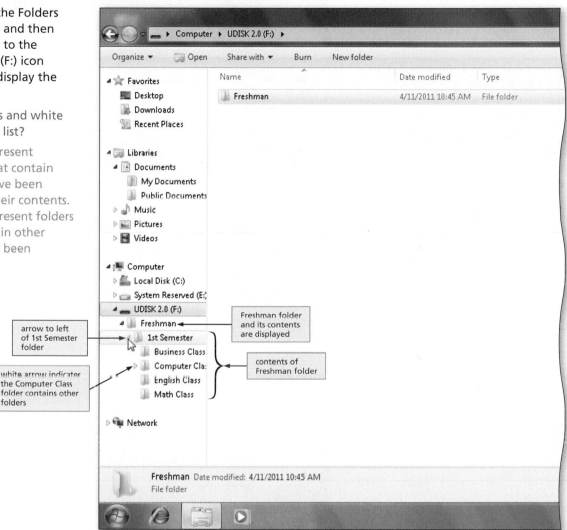

Figure 56

Other Ways
1. Double-click drive icon in Folders list
2. Select drive to expand using arrow keys, press RIGHT ARROW on keyboard
3. Select drive to expand, press RIGHT ARROW

To Collapse a Folder

When a black arrow is displayed to the left of a folder icon in the Folders list, the folder is expanded and shows all the folders it contains. The following step collapses the 1st Semester folder.

- Click the black arrow to the left of the 1st Semester folder icon in the Folders list to collapse the 1st Semester folder (Figure 57).

Q&A

Why is the 1st Semester folder indented below the Freshman folder in the Folders list?

The folder is indented below the Freshman icon to show that the folder is contained within the Freshman folder.

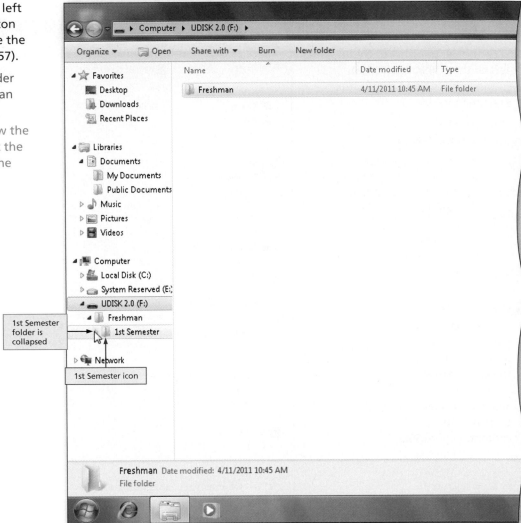

Figure 57

Other Ways

1. Double-click folder icon in Folders list
2. Select folder to collapse using arrow keys, press LEFT ARROW on keyboard
3. Select folder to collapse, press LEFT ARROW

To Display the Contents of a Folder

Clicking a folder icon in the Folders list displays the contents of the drive or folder in the right pane and displays the path in the Address bar. The following step displays the contents of the 1st Semester folder.

1

• Click the 1st Semester icon in the Folders list to display the contents of the 1st Semester folder in the File list (Figure 58).

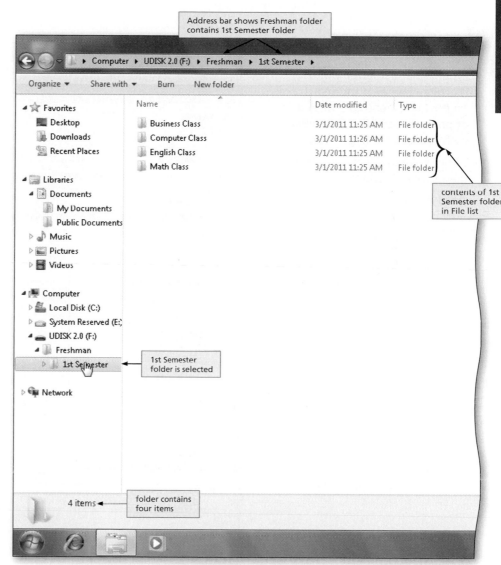

Figure 58

Creating a Document and Folder Using WordPad

The Freshman folder was created on the UDISK 2.0 (F:) drive when you downloaded the files. You also can create a folder anytime you save a file in a Windows program. For example, you can use WordPad to create a document and then save the new document in a folder. **WordPad** is a basic word processing program included with Windows 7 that allows you to create a variety of personal and business documents. As one of the programs in the Accessories list, one method to start WordPad is to display the Start menu, click All Programs, click Accessories, and click WordPad in the Accessories list.

An easier method to start WordPad is to use the Search box on the Start menu. The Search box allows you to find a specific program, file, e-mail message, or Internet favorite by typing the first few letters in the Search box at the bottom of the Start menu.

To Start WordPad Using the Search Box

Assume you want to create a WordPad document that lists your homework for Friday, April 11. The first step is to start the WordPad program using the Search box. The following steps find and then start WordPad using the Search box at the bottom of the Start menu.

- Display the Start menu.

- Type w (the first letter in the WordPad name) in the Search box on the Start menu to display a list of programs and files beginning with the letter w (Figure 59).

Q&A

What is displayed on the Start menu when I type the letter w?

A list of programs and files that begin with the letter entered, w, are displayed. As you type the entire program name, fewer selections remain in the list until you find your selection or no items match your search term.

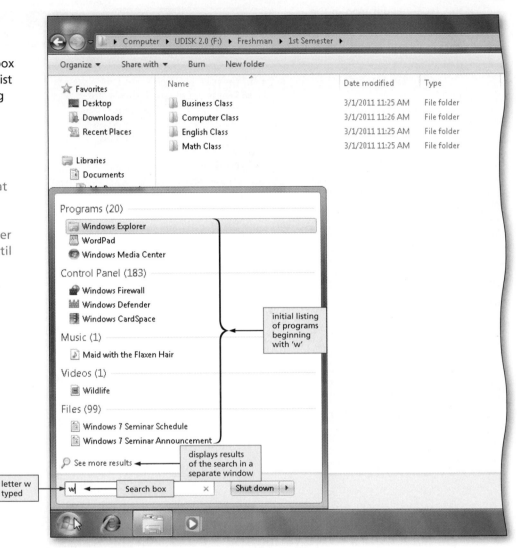

Figure 59

②

• Type the letter o (the second letter in the WordPad name) in the Search box on the Start menu to refine the list of search results (Figure 60).

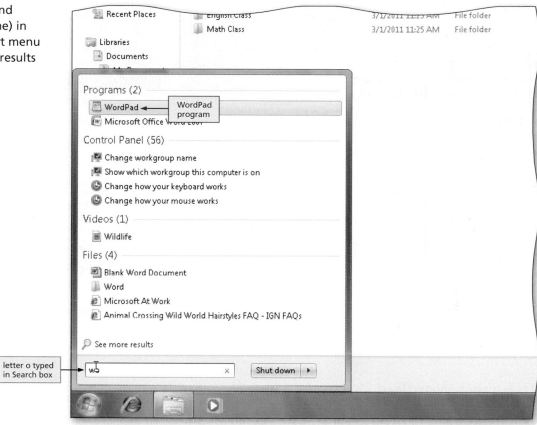

Figure 60

③

• Click WordPad in the search results to start the WordPad program and display a new WordPad document (Figure 61).

• If the WordPad window is not maximized, click the Maximize button on the title bar to maximize the window.

Q&A

Could I continue typing the remainder of the letters in the WordPad name?

Yes, but to start the program you still need to click WordPad in the search results.

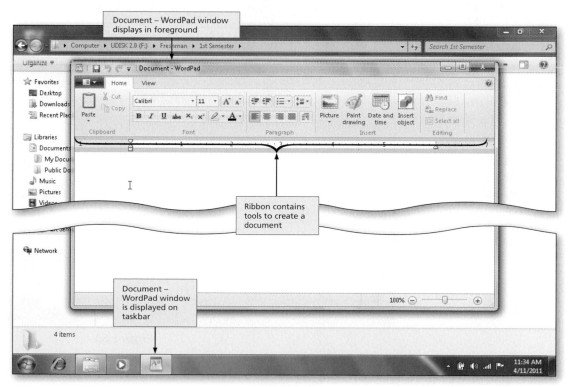

Figure 61

To Type Text

After starting WordPad, you can enter the text for a new document. The following step enters text in the new WordPad document.

• Type Friday, April 11 and then press the ENTER key twice.

• Type Finish - The Bike Delivers Database and then press the ENTER key.

• Type Read - Next Project and then press the ENTER key (Figure 62).

Q&A

What if I make an error while typing?

You can press the BACKSPACE key to delete the error and then retype the text correctly.

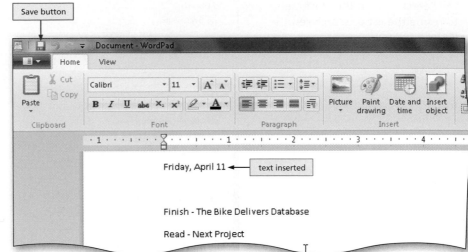

Figure 62

To Save a WordPad Document in a New Folder

After typing the text of your WordPad document, you can create a new folder, and then save the document in the created folder. The following steps save the new document with the file name Friday, April 11 in a new folder named Homework. The Homework folder is created within the Computer Class folder (see the hierarchy in Figure 50 on page WIN 36).

• Click the Save button on the Quick Launch toolbar to display the Save As dialog box.

• If necessary, double-click the Save As dialog box title bar to maximize the Save As dialog box (Figure 63).

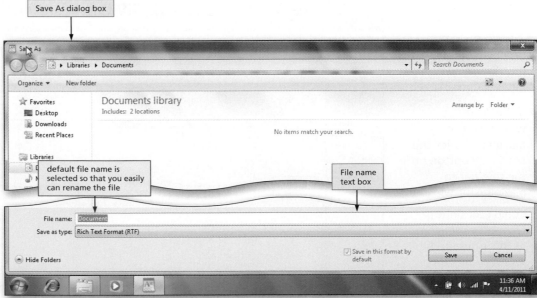

Figure 63

②

- Type Friday, April 11 in the File name text box. Do not press the ENTER key after typing the file name (Figure 64).

Q&A What happens if I press the ENTER key after typing the file name?

If you press the ENTER key, the Save As dialog box closes and the file is saved to the default save location. In this case, the file will be saved to the Documents folder, which is the default save location within the Documents library. If you want to save the file in a folder other than the Documents folder, you must select the desired folder before clicking the Save button.

Q&A What if the Navigation pane does not appear in the Save As dialog box?

Click the Browse Folders button.

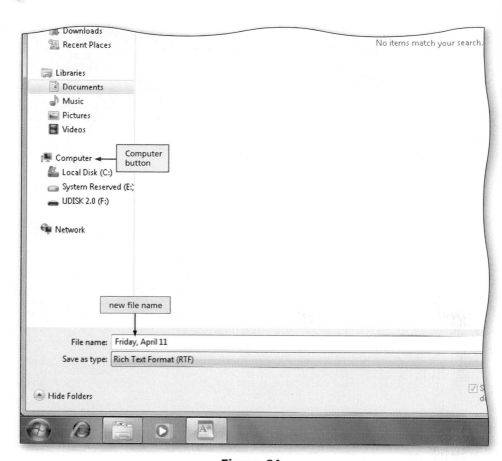

Figure 64

③

- If necessary, click the arrow to the left of Computer in the left pane to expand the Computer list (Figure 65).

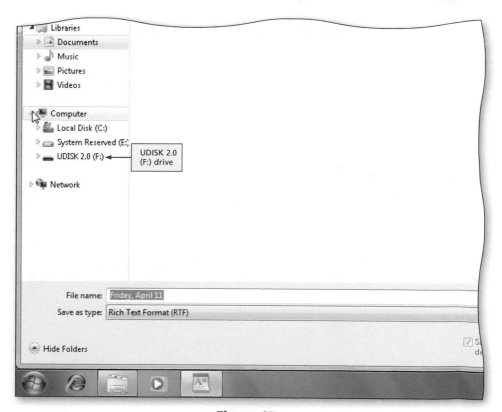

Figure 65

4

- Click UDISK 2.0 (F:) in the Computer list to display the contents of the UDISK 2.0 (F:) folder in the right pane (Figure 66).

Q&A Why is my list of drives and folders different from the one in Figure 66?

Folders and drives can be unique for each computer.

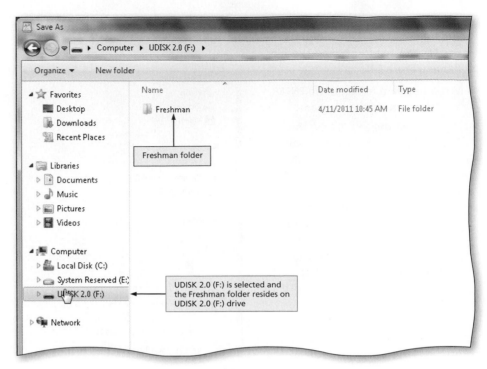

Figure 66

5

- Double-click the Freshman folder in the right pane in the Save As dialog box to display the 1st Semester folder (Figure 67).

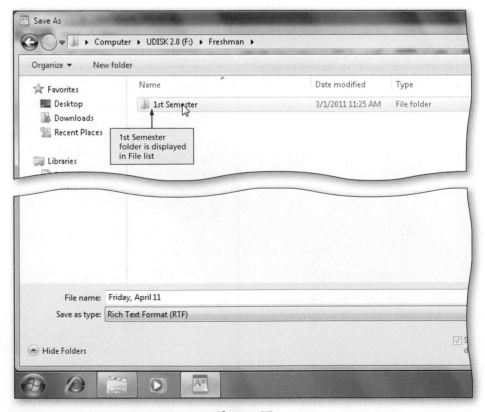

Figure 67

6
• Double-click the 1st Semester folder in the Save As dialog box to display the contents of the 1st Semester folder (Figure 68).

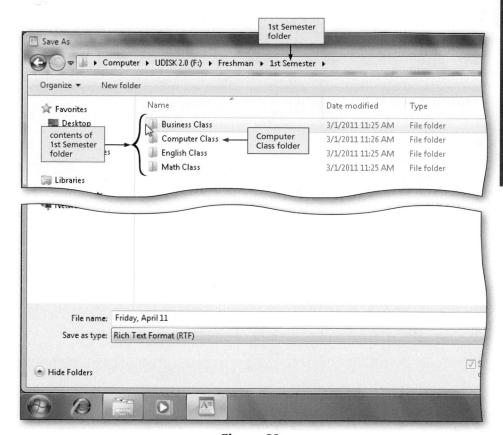

Figure 68

7
• Double-click the Computer Class folder in the Save As dialog box to display its contents (Figure 69).

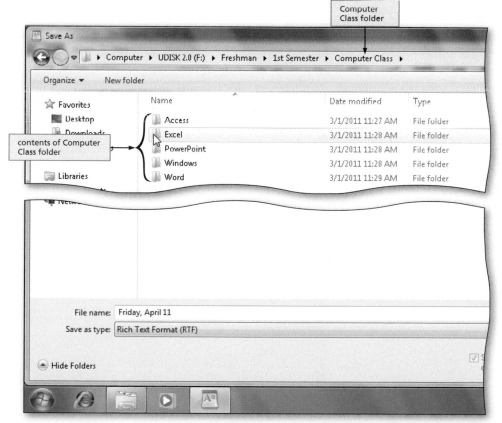

Figure 69

- Click the New folder button in the Save As dialog box to create a new folder within the Computer Class folder.

- Type Homework as the name of the folder and then press the ENTER key two times (Figure 70).

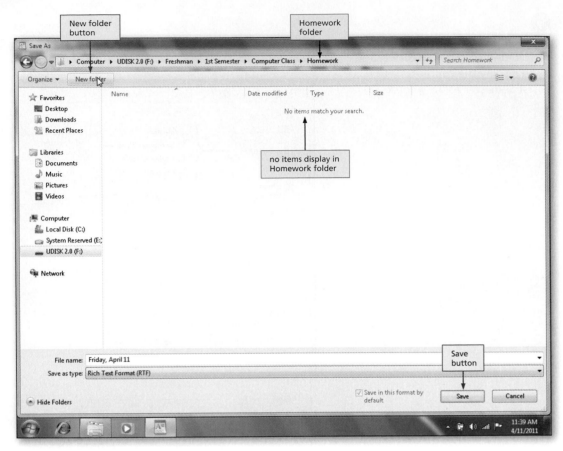

Figure 70

- Click the Save button in the Save As dialog box to save the Friday, April 11 document to its new location in the Homework folder (Figure 71).

- Click the Close button on the WordPad title bar to close the window.

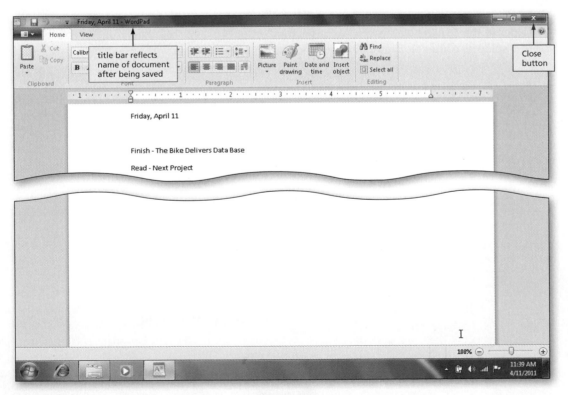

Figure 71

To Verify the Contents of a Folder

After saving the Friday, April 11 document in the Homework folder, you can verify that the document was correctly saved in the Homework folder. The following step verifies the Homework folder contains the Friday, April 11 document.

- Click the white arrow next to the 1st Semester icon in the Computer list to display the folders within the 1st Semester folder.

- Click the white arrow next to the Computer Class icon in the Folders list to display the folders within the Computer Class folder.

- Click the Homework icon in the Folders list to select the Homework folder and display the contents of the Homework folder in the right pane (Figure 72).

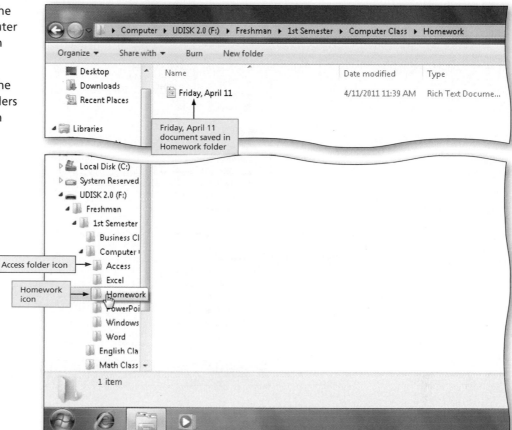

Figure 72

File Management

Being able to manage the files on the computer is one of the most important computer skills. **File management** includes copying, moving, renaming, and deleting files and folders on the computer. When copying files, the drive and folder containing the files to be copied are called the **source drive** and **source folder**, respectively. The drive and folder to which the files are copied are called the **destination drive** and **destination folder**, respectively.

To Copy a File by Right-Dragging

The steps on the following pages show one method of copying files — right-drag a file icon from the right pane to a folder or drive icon in the left pane. These steps copy the The Bike Delivers file from the Access folder (source folder) to the Homework (destination folder). The UDISK 2.0 (F:) drive is both the source drive and the destination drive.

- Click the Access folder icon in the Computer list to select the Access folder and display its contents in the right pane (Figure 73).

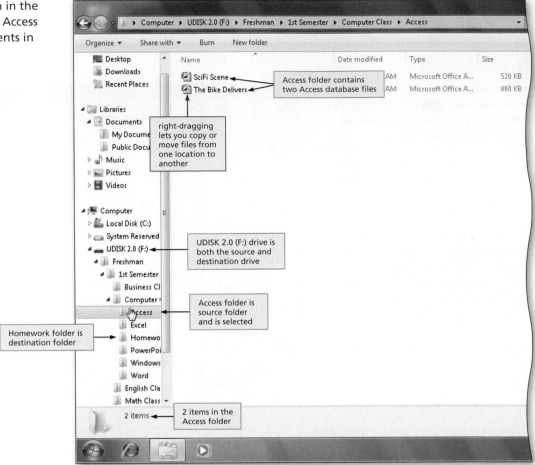

Figure 73

- Right-drag the The Bike Delivers icon from the right pane to the Homework folder icon in the Folders list to display the shortcut menu (Figure 74).

Q&A

What should I do if I right-drag a file to the wrong folder?

Click Cancel on the shortcut menu and then right-drag the file to the correct folder.

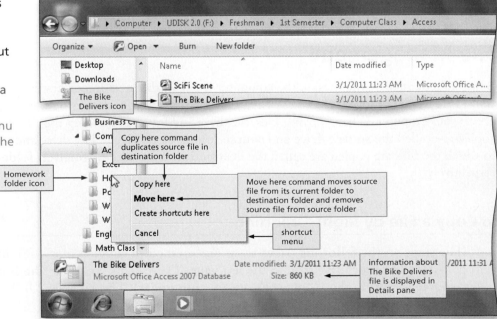

Figure 74

• Click Copy here on the shortcut menu to copy the The Bike
Delivers file to the Homework
folder (Figure 75).

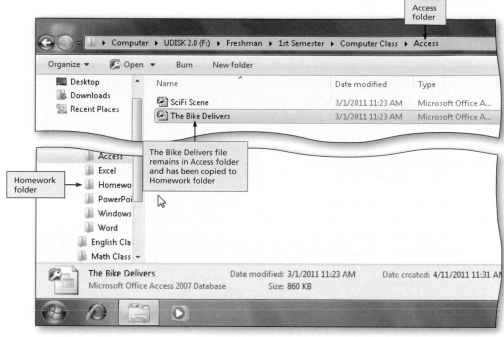

Figure 75

Other Ways

1. Right-click file to copy,
   click Copy on shortcut
   menu, right-click
   Homework folder, click
   Paste on shortcut menu
2. Select file to copy,
   press CTRL+C, select
   Homework folder,
   press CTRL+V

To Display the Contents of a Folder

After copying a file, you might want to examine the folder or drive where the file
was copied to ensure it was copied properly. The following step displays the contents of
the Homework folder.

• Click the Homework folder in the Computer list to display the contents of the Homework
folder (Figure 76).

Q&A

Can I copy or move more than one
file at a time?

Yes. To copy or move multiple files,
select each file to be copied or
moved by clicking the file icon while
holding down the CTRL key. Then,
right-drag the selected files to the
destination folder using the same
technique as right-dragging a single
file.

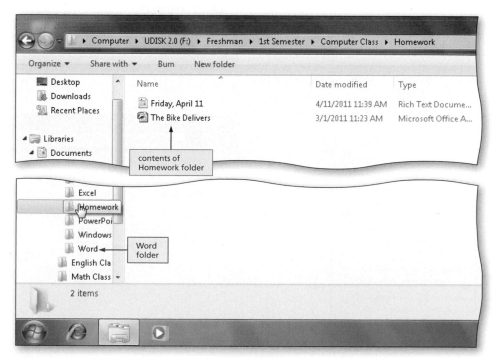

Figure 76

To Rename a File

In some circumstances, you may want to rename a file or a folder. This could occur when you want to distinguish a file in one folder or drive from a copy, or if you decide you need a more descriptive name to identify a file. The Word folder in Figure 77 contains the three Word documents (Barn and Silo, Fall Harvest, and Lake at Sunset). In this case, you decide to change the Fall Harvest name to Great Fall Harvest. The following steps change the name of the Fall Harvest file in the Word folder to Great Fall Harvest.

- Click the Word folder in the left pane to display the three files it contains in the right pane.

- Right-click the Fall Harvest icon in the right pane to select the Fall Harvest icon and display a short-cut menu (Figure 77). Depending upon your computer's configu-ration, the commands on your shortcut menu might differ.

- Click Rename on the shortcut menu to select the file name for renaming.

- Type `Great Fall Harvest` and then press the ENTER key (Figure 78).

Q&A

Are any risks involved in renaming files?

If you inadvertently rename a file or change its file extension, the programs might not be able to find the file and, therefore, might not execute properly. Always use caution when renaming files.

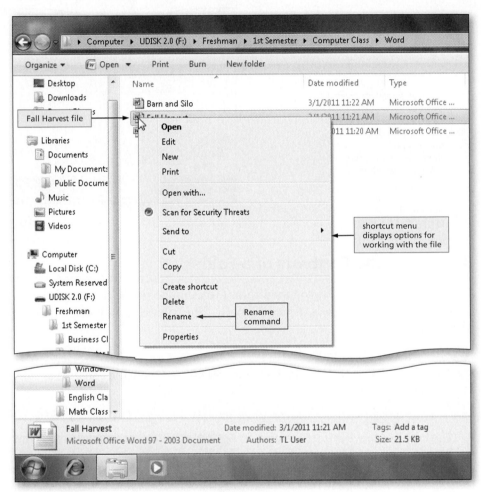

Figure 77

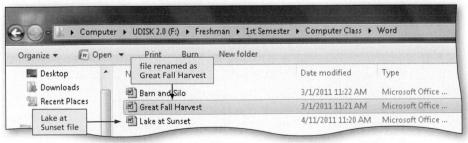

Figure 78

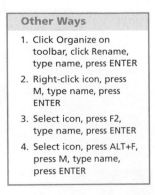

Other Ways

1. Click Organize on toolbar, click Rename, type name, press ENTER

2. Right-click icon, press M, type name, press ENTER

3. Select icon, press F2, type name, press ENTER

4. Select icon, press ALT+F, press M, type name, press ENTER

To Delete a File by Right-Clicking

A final task you will want to perform is to delete a file. Exercise caution when deleting a file or files. When you delete a file from a hard disk, the deleted file is stored in the Recycle Bin where you can recover it until you empty the Recycle Bin. If you delete a file from removable media, the file is gone permanently once you delete it. The following steps delete the Lake at Sunset file.

- Right-click the Lake at Sunset icon in the right pane to select the icon and display a shortcut menu (Figure 79).

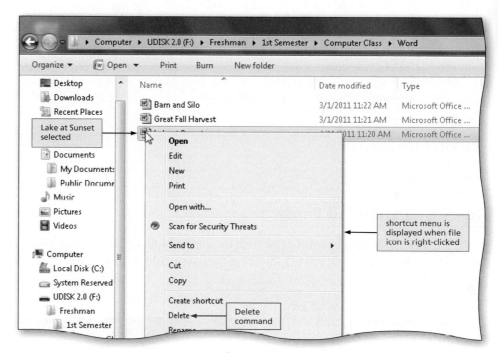

Figure 79

- Click Delete on the shortcut menu to display the Delete File dialog box (Figure 80).

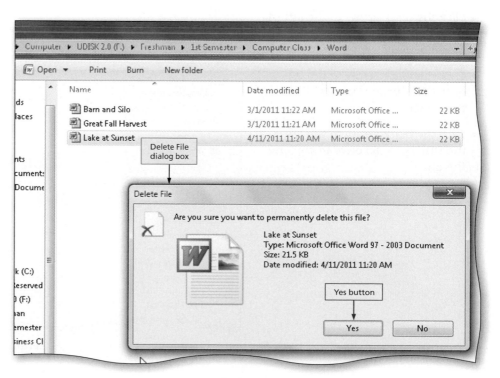

Figure 80

• Click the Yes button in the Delete File dialog box to delete the Lake at Sunset file (Figure 81).

Q&A

Can I use this same technique to delete a folder?

Yes. Right-click the folder and then click Delete on the shortcut menu. When you delete a folder, all the files and folders contained in the folder you are deleting, together with any files and folders on lower hierarchical levels, are deleted as well.

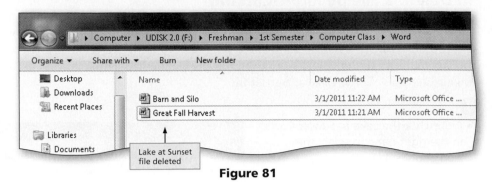

Figure 81

Other Ways

1. Select icon, press ALT+F, press D, press Y

To Close Expanded Folders

After you have completed work with expanded folders, you will want to close the expanded folders. The following steps close the Computer Class folder, 1st Semester folder, Freshman folder, and UDISK 2.0 (F:) drive.

• Click the black arrow to the left of the Computer Class folder in the left pane to collapse the Computer Class folder (Figure 82).

• Click the black arrow to the left of the 1st Semester folder to collapse the folder.

• Click the black arrow to the left of the Freshman folder to collapse the folder.

• Click the black arrow to the left of the UDISK 2.0 (F:) drive to collapse the drive.

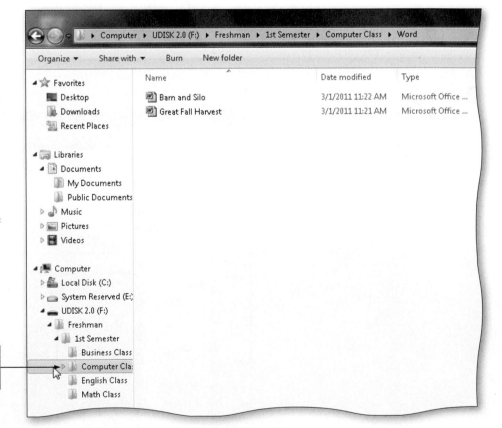

Figure 82

Other Ways

1. Click expanded folder icon, press LEFT ARROW

To Close the Computer Window

When you have finished working, you can remove the USB flash drive and close the Computer window. The following steps close the Computer window.

1 Click the Computer button on the Address bar to display the contents of the computer.

2 If necessary, click the UDISK (F:) icon to select it.

3 Click the Eject button on the toolbar to prepare the USB flash drive to be safely removed from the computer.

4 Remove the USB flash drive from the USB port.

5 Cick the Close button on the title bar to close the window.

Using Help and Support

One of the more powerful Windows 7 features is Windows Help and Support. **Windows Help and Support** is available when using Windows 7, or when using any program running under Windows 7. It contains answers to many questions you might have concerning the Windows 7 operating system.

To Start Windows Help and Support

Before you can access the Windows Help and Support services, you must start Help and Support. One method of starting Help and Support uses the Start menu. The following steps open the Windows Help and Support window.

1
• Display the Start menu (Figure 83).

Figure 83

2

- Click Help and Support to display the Windows Help and Support window.

- If necessary, click the Maximize button on the Windows Help and Support title bar to maximize the Windows Help and Support window (Figure 84).

Q&A

What does Windows Help and Support contain?

Windows Help and Support contains a title bar, navigation toolbar, 'Find an answer quickly' area, 'Not sure where to start?' area, and 'More on the Windows website' area.

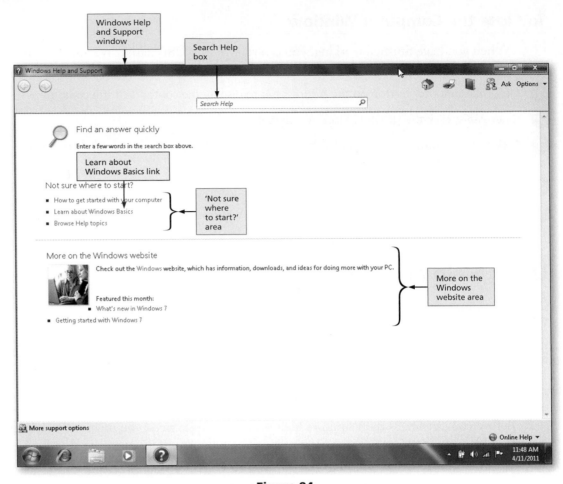

Figure 84

Other Ways

1. Press CTRL+ESC, press RIGHT ARROW, press UP ARROW, press ENTER
2. Press WINDOWS+F1

Table 4 shows the content areas in the Windows Help and Support Center.

Table 4 Windows Help and Support Center Content Areas	
Area	**Function**
Find an answer quickly	This area contains instructions about how to perform a quick search using the Search Help box.
Not sure where to start?	This area displays three links to topics to help guide users: How to get started with your computer, Learn about Windows Basics, and Browse Help topics. Clicking one of the options takes you to corresponding Help and Support pages.
More on the Windows website	This area contains links to online content from the Windows Web site. Clicking one of the links takes you to the corresponding Web pages on the Web site.

To Browse for Help Topics in Windows Basics

After starting Windows Help and Support, the next action is to find the Help topic in which you are interested. The following steps use the 'Not sure where to start?' area in Windows Help and Support to find a Help topic that describes how to use the Windows Help and Support.

- Click Learn about Windows Basics in the 'Not sure where to start?' area to display the Windows Basics: all topics heading (Figure 85).

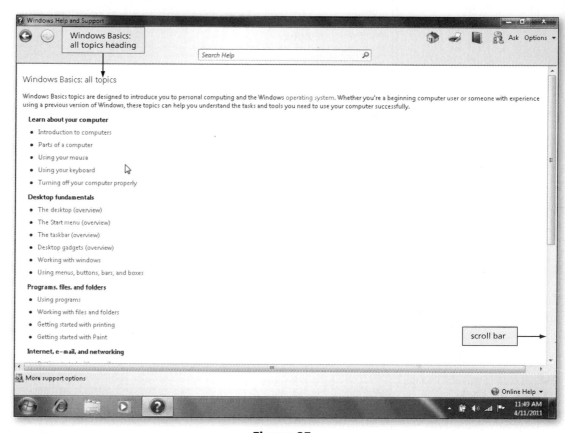

Figure 85

- Scroll down to view the Getting help topic (Figure 86).

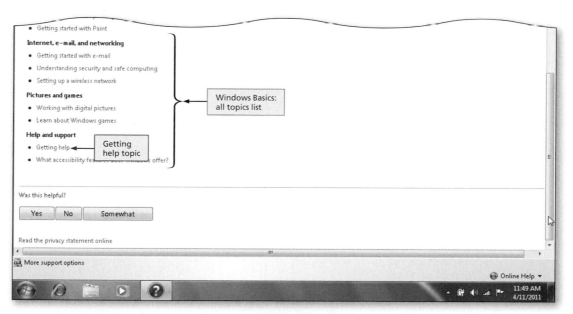

Figure 86

3

- Click the Getting help link (Figure 87).

- Read the information in the Getting help topic.

Getting help topic

Back button

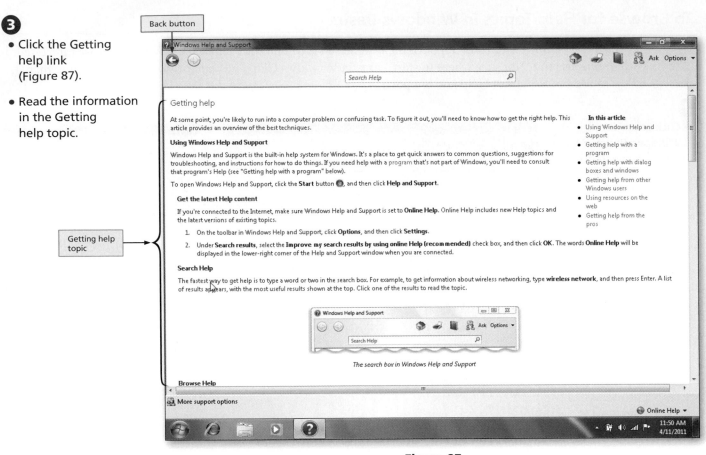

Figure 87

4

- Click the Back button on the Navigation bar two times to return to the Help home page (Figure 88).

clicking Back button twice returns you to the Help home page

Browse Help topics link

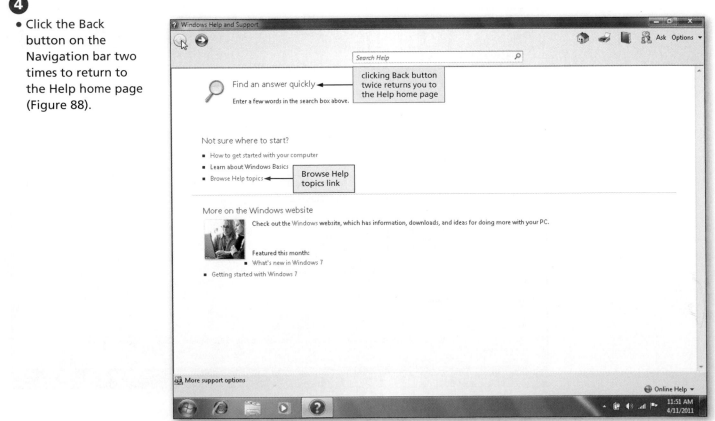

Figure 88

To Search for Help Topics Using the Contents Page

A second method of finding answers to your questions about Windows 7 is to use the Browse Help topics link in the 'Not sure where to start?' area. The **Contents page** contains a list of entries organized as a table of contents, where, each entry references one or more Help topics. The following steps obtain help and information about what you need to set up a home network.

1

• Click the Browse Help topics link in the 'Not sure where to start?' area to display the Contents page (Figure 89).

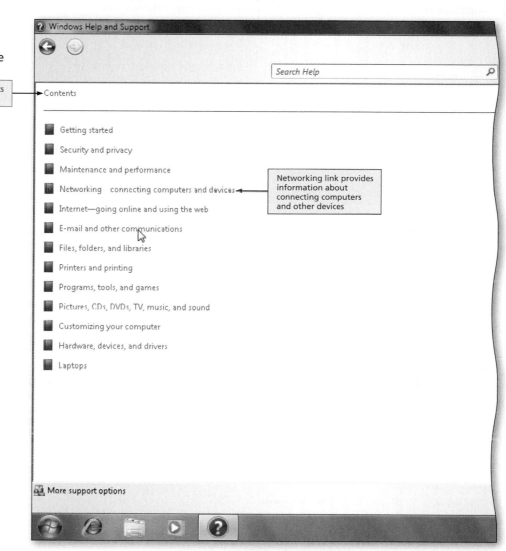

Figure 89

2

- Click the 'Networking — connecting computers and devices' link in the Contents area (Figure 90).

Q&A What happens if the topic I am interested in is not included in the table of contents?

Type the term in the Search Help text box in the Windows Help and Support window, and then press the ENTER key to find information about your topic.

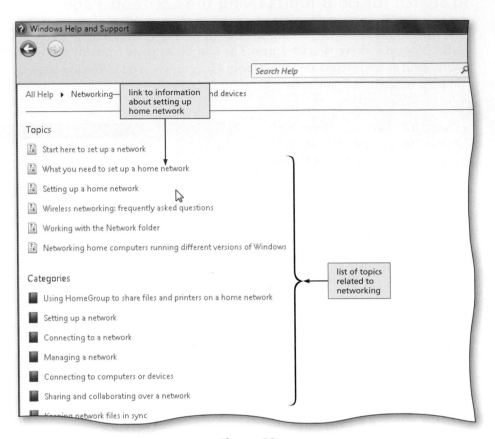

Figure 90

3

- Click the 'What you need to set up a home network' link (Figure 91).

- Read the information about what you need to set up a home network.

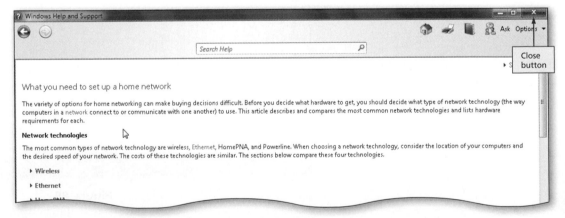

Figure 91

To Close Windows Help and Support

The following step closes the Windows Help and Support window.

1 Close the Windows Help and Support window.

Logging Off and Turning Off the Computer

After completing your work with Windows 7, you should close your user account by logging off the computer. In addition to logging off, there are several options available for ending a Windows 7 session. Table 5 illustrates the various options for ending your Windows 7 session.

Table 5 Options and Methods for Ending a Windows Vista Session	
Option	**Description**
Switch user	Click the Start button, point to the arrow next to the Shut down button, and then click Switch user to keep your programs running in the background (but inaccessible until you log on again), and allow another user to log on.
Log off	Click the Start button, point to the arrow next to the Shut down button, and then click Log off to close all your programs and close your user account. This method leaves the computer running so that another user can log on.
Lock	Click the Start button, point to the arrow next to the Shut down button, and then click Lock to deny anyone except those who have authorized access to log on the computer.
Restart	Click the Start button, point to the arrow next to the Shut down button, and then click Restart to close all open programs, log off, and restart the computer.
Sleep	Click the Start button, point to the arrow next to the Shut down button, click Sleep, wait for Windows to save your work to memory and then power down your computer to a low-power state. This is useful if you are expecting to return to your computer in a short amount of time.
Hibernate	Click the Start button, point to the arrow next to the Shut down button, and then click Hibernate. Windows will save your session to the hard disk and turn off your computer. When you turn the computer on again, Windows restores your session. This is useful if you are expecting to not use your computer for at least several hours.
Shut down	Click the Start button and then click the Shut down button to close all your programs and turn off the computer.

To Log Off the Computer

Logging off the computer closes any open programs, allows you to save any unsaved documents, ends the Windows 7 session, and makes the computer available for other users. The following steps log off the computer.

1

• Display the Start menu (Figure 92).

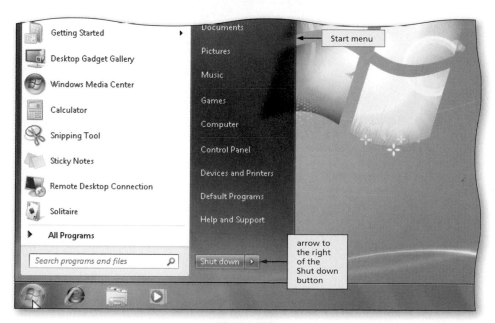

Figure 92

- Click the arrow to the right of the Shut down button to display the Shut down menu (Figure 93).

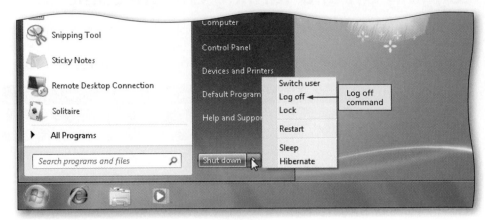

Figure 93

- Click Log Off to log off (Figure 94).

Q&A

Why should I log off the computer?

It is important to log off the computer so that you do not lose your work. Some users of Windows 7 have turned off their computers without following the log off procedure only to find they had lost data they thought they had stored on the hard disk.

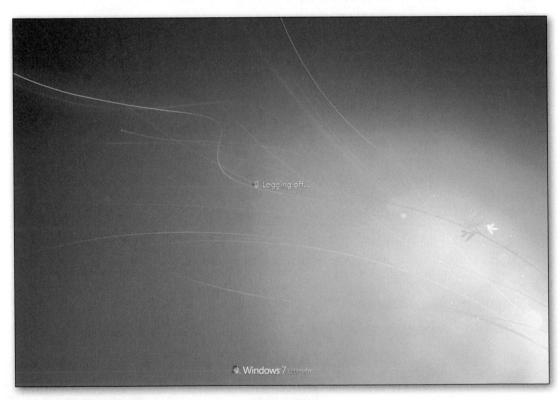

Figure 94

To Turn Off the Computer

After logging off, you also may want to shut down the computer using the Shut down button or the 'Shut down options' button in the lower corner of the Welcome screen. Clicking the left button shuts down your computer, and clicking the right button displays a menu containing three commands (Restart, Sleep, and Shut down) that can be used to restart the computer, put the computer into sleep mode, and shut down the computer. The following step turns off the computer. If you are not sure whether you should turn off the computer, simply read the step without performing it.

• Click the Shut down button on the Welcome screen to shut down the computer.

Other Ways
1. Press ALT+F4, press DOWN ARROW, select Shut Down, click OK

Chapter Summary

In this chapter, you learned about the different Windows 7 editions and Windows 7 graphical interface. You started Windows 7, learned the components of the desktop and basic mouse operations. You opened, closed, moved, resized, minimized, maximized, and scrolled a window. You expanded and collapsed drives and folders, displayed drive and folder contents, created a folder, copied a file between folders, and renamed and then deleted a file. You used Internet Explorer to browse the World Wide Web using a Web address and tabs. You learned about hierarchical folder organization, USB flash drives, and you used WordPad to create and save a document in a newly created folder. You searched for files by typing a word in the Search box, you obtained Help using Windows 7, and shut down Windows 7.

1. Log On the Computer (WIN 8)
2. Add a Gadget to the Desktop (WIN 10)
3. Remove a Gadget from the Desktop (WIN 12)
4. Display the Start Menu (WIN 13)
5. Scroll Using Scroll Arrows, the Scroll Bar, and the Scroll Box (WIN 15)
6. Add an Icon to the Desktop (WIN 16)
7. Open a Window Using a Desktop Icon (WIN 18)
8. Minimize and Redisplay a Window (WIN 19)
9. Maximize and Restore a Window (WIN 20)
10. Close a Window (WIN 21)
11. Open a Window Using the Start Menu (WIN 21)
12. Move a Window by Dragging (WIN 22)
13. Expand the Local Disk (C:) List (WIN 23)
14. Size a Window by Dragging (WIN 23)
15. Collapse the Local Disk (C:) List (WIN 24)
16. Delete a Desktop Icon by Right-Dragging (WIN 25)
17. Start a Program Using the Start Menu (WIN 27)
18. Browse the Web by Entering a Web Address (WIN 30)
19. Open a Link on a New Tab (WIN 31)
20. Switch between Tabs (WIN 33)

21. Close a Tab (WIN 33)
22. Display the Computer Window (WIN 34)
23. Create a Folder on a USB Flash Drive (WIN 38)
24. Download a Hierarchy of Folders into the Freshman Folder (WIN 39)
25. Expand a Drive and its content (WIN 41)
26. Collapse a Folder (WIN 42)
27. Display the Contents of a Folder (WIN 43)
28. Start WordPad Using the Search Box (WIN 44)
29. Type Text (WIN 46)
30. Save a WordPad Document in a New Folder (WIN 46)
31. Verify the Contents of a Folder (WIN 51)
32. Copy a File by Right-Dragging (WIN 51)
33. Rename a File (WIN 54)
34. Delete a File by Right-Clicking (WIN 55)
35. Close Expanded Folders (WIN 56)
36. Start Windows Help and Support (WIN 57)
37. Browse for Help Topics in Windows Basics (WIN 59)
38. Search for Help Topics Using the Table of Contents (WIN 61)
39. Log Off the Computer (WIN 63)
40. Turn Off the Computer (WIN 65)

Learn It Online

Test your knowledge of chapter content and key terms.

Instructions: To complete the Learn It Online exercises, start your browser, click the Address bar, and then enter the Web address scsite.com/win7/learn. When the Windows Learn It Online page is displayed, click the link for the exercise you want to complete and then read the instructions.

Chapter Reinforcement TF, MC, and SA
A series of true/false, multiple choice, and short answer questions that test your knowledge of the chapter content.

Flash Cards
An interactive learning environment where you identify chapter key terms associated with displayed definitions.

Practice Test
A series of multiple choice questions that test your knowledge of chapter content and key terms.

Who Wants To Be a Computer Genius?
An interactive game that challenges your knowledge of chapter content in the style of a television quiz show.

Wheel of Terms
An interactive game that challenges your knowledge of chapter key terms in the style of the television show *Wheel of Fortune*.

Crossword Puzzle Challenge
A crossword puzzle that challenges your knowledge of key terms presented in the chapter.

In the Lab

Using the guidelines, concepts, and skills presented in this chapter, complete the following Labs.

Lab 1: Improving Your Mouse Skills with Windows Gadgets
Instructions: Perform the following steps to play a game using a gadget.
1. Open the Start menu and then open All Programs. Click Desktop Gadget Gallery. Double-click the Picture Puzzle to add it to the desktop. Close the Gadget Gallery window.
2. Click the Show picture button on the Picture Puzzle to see what the picture will look like once you solve the puzzle (Figure 95).
3. Play the Picture Puzzle game, by moving the puzzle tiles around by clicking on them when they are near the empty slot. Continue to rearrange the tiles until you have completed the picture (you can show the picture at any time to determine if you are close to the solution). Record your time here:

_____

4. Click the Close button on the gadget to remove the gadget from the desktop.

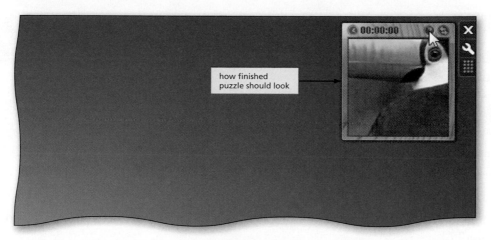

how finished
puzzle should look

Figure 95

In the Lab

Lab 2: Internet Explorer

Instructions: Use a computer to perform the following tasks.

1. Start Windows 7.

2. Click the Internet Explorer icon on the taskbar to start Internet Explorer. What is the Web address of the Web page that appears in the Address bar in the Windows Internet Explorer window? _____

3. Click the Web address in the Address bar in the Windows Internet Explorer window to select it. Type scsite.com and then press the ENTER key.

4. If necessary, scroll the Web page to display the Browse by Subject navigation bar containing the subject categories. Clicking a subject category displays the book titles in that category.

5. Click Operating Systems in the Browse by Subject navigation bar.

6. Click the Windows 7 link.

7. Right-click the first Windows 7 textbook cover image on the Web page, click Save Picture As on the shortcut menu, type Windows 7 Cover in the File name text box, and then click the Save button in the Save Picture dialog box to save the image in the Pictures library.

8. Close Internet Explorer.

9. Display the Start menu. Click Pictures to display the Pictures library. If necessary, maximize the Pictures library.

10. Right-click the Windows 7 Cover icon and then click Properties on the shortcut menu.

   a.   What type of file is the Windows 7 Cover file? _____

   b.   When was the file last modified? _____

   c.   With what program does this file open? _____

11. Click the Cancel button in the Windows 7 Cover Properties dialog box.

12. Insert a USB flash drive to one of your computer's USB ports. If necessary, close the Auto Play window.

13. Right-drag the Windows 7 Cover icon to the USB flash drive icon in the Folders list. Click Move Here on the shortcut menu. Click the USB flash drive icon in the Folders list.

   a.   Is the Windows 7 Cover file stored on the USB flash drive? _____

14. Close the USB flash drive window.

15. Eject the USB flash drive.

In the Lab

Lab 3: Getting Help

Instructions: Use a computer to perform the following tasks.

Part 1:   Using Windows Basics to Get Help

1. If necessary, start Windows 7 and then log on the computer.

2. Display the Start menu and then click Help and Support.

3. If necessary, maximize the Windows Help and Support window.

4. Click Learn about Windows Basics link in the 'Not sure where to start?' area.

5. Click the 'Turning off your computer properly' link. What are the three ways to turn off your computer?

   _____

   _____

6. Click the Back button in the upper-left corner of the Windows Help and Support window.

7. Click the 'Getting started with printing' link below the Programs, files, and folders' heading. List the three types of printers and the most common type of printer connections.

   _____

8. Click the Back button in the upper-left corner of the Windows Help and Support window.

9. If necessary, scroll to view the Getting help topic below the 'Help and support' heading. Click the Getting help link. List the different ways you can get help.

   _____

   _____

10. Click the Back button twice to return to the Windows Help and Support home page.

Part 2:   Browsing Help topics to Get Help

1. Click the 'Browse Help topics' link in the 'Not sure where to start?' area.

2. Click the 'E-mail and other communications' link. Click the 'When to trust an e-mail message' link. List the questions that can help you decide whether you should trust an e-mail message or attachment.

   _____

   _____

3. Click Windows Contacts (address book) in the Categories list.

4. Click the 'Managing your contacts' in the Contents list.

5. List the different types of information that can be stored in a contact.

   _____

   _____

6. Click the Back button three times to return to the Contents page.

7. Click the Security and privacy link in the Contents list.

8. What is the Action Center?

   _____

   _____

9. Why is keeping Windows up to date important?

_____

_____

10. Click the Help home button (the icon looks like a house) to return to the Windows Help and Support home page.

Part 3:   Using Search to Get Help

1. Click the Search Help text box, type `connect to the Internet`, and then press the ENTER key.

2. Click the 'What do I need to connect to the Internet?' link.

3. What tools and services do you use to connect to the Internet?

_____

4. Click the Back button three times in the upper-left corner of the Windows Help and Support.

Part 4:   Using Windows Online Help to Get Help

1. Click the Windows link in the 'More on the Windows website' area to open the Windows home page in Internet Explorer.

2. Click the Windows 7 link under the Help & How-to heading to display the Windows 7 Help & How-to page.

3. Click the 'Personalize your PC' link.

4. What can you do in the Personalize your PC area in the Windows Help and How-to Web site?

_____

_____

5. Close the Personalizing your computer window and then close the Windows Help and Support window.

Cases and Places

Apply your creative thinking and problem-solving skills to design and implement a solution.

• Easier   •• More Difficult

• 1: Researching Technical Support

Technical support is an important consideration when installing and using an operating system or a program. The ability to obtain a valid answer to a question at the moment you have the question can be the difference between a frustrating incident and a positive experience. Using Windows Help and Support, the Internet, or another research facility, write a brief report on the options that are available for obtaining help and technical support while using Windows 7.

• 2: Assessing Windows 7 Compatibility

The Windows 7 operating system can be installed only on computers found in the Windows 7 hardware compatibility list. Locate three older personal computers. Look for them in your school's computer lab, at a local business, or in your house. Use the Windows Web site on the Internet to locate the Windows 7 Compatibility Center. Check each computer against the list and write a brief report summarizing your results.

•• 3: Researching Multiple Operating Systems

Using the Internet, a library, or other research facility, write a brief report on the Windows, Mac OS, and Linux operating systems. Describe the systems, pointing out their similarities and differences. Discuss the advantages and disadvantages of each. Finally, tell which operating system you would purchase and explain why.

•• 4: Sharing Your Pictures

Make It Personal

Using Windows Help and Support and the keywords, digital pictures, locate the "Working with Digital Pictures" article. In a brief report, summarize the steps required to send a photo in an e-mail message as well as the different ways to get photos from your camera. Next, research Windows Live Essentials and include a description of how to organize and find your pictures.

•• 5: Researching Operating Systems in Use

Working Together

Because of the many important tasks an operating system performs, most businesses put a great deal of thought into choosing an operating system. Each team member should interview a person at a local business about the operating system he or she uses with his or her computers. Based on the interview, write a brief report on why the businesses chose that operating system, how satisfied it is with it, and under what circumstances it might consider switching to a different operating system.

Appendix A
Comparison of the New Features of Windows 7 Editions

The Microsoft Windows 7 operating system is available in a variety of editions. The six editions that you most likely will encounter are Windows 7 Starter, Windows 7 Home Basic, Windows 7 Home Premium, Windows 7 Professional, Windows 7 Enterprise, and Windows 7 Ultimate. Because not all computers have the same hardware or are used for the same functions, Microsoft provides these various editions so that each user can have the edition that meets his or her needs. Table A–1 compares features in the various editions. Windows 7 Ultimate, the most complete version of Windows 7, is used as a baseline for clarifying the features of the other editions. Windows 7 Starter and Windows 7 Home Basic are not included in this table as they are more limited in their offerings.

Table A–1 Comparison of Windows 7 Editions

Ultimate Features	Home Premium	Professional	Enterprise
64-bit Support	✓	✓	✓
Action Center	✓	✓	✓
Aero Peek	✓	✓	✓
Aero Shake	✓	✓	✓
Backup and Restore	✓	✓	✓
BitLocker			✓
DirectX 11	✓	✓	✓
Domain Join		✓	✓
HomeGroup	✓	✓	✓
Internet Explorer 8	✓	✓	✓
Jump Lists	✓	✓	✓
Libraries	✓	✓	✓
Location Aware Printing		✓	✓
Maximum RAM (32-bit)	4 GB	4 GB	4 GB
Maximum RAM (64-bit)	16 GB	192 GB	192 GB
Minimum RAM (32-bit)	1 GB	1 GB	1 GB
Minimum RAM (64-bit)	2 GB	2 GB	2 GB
Multiplayer Games	✓	✓	✓

Table A–1 Comparison of Windows 7 Editions *(continued)*

Ultimate Features	Home Premium	Professional	Enterprise
Parental Controls	✓	✓	✓
Pin	✓	✓	✓
Play To	✓	✓	✓
Power Management	✓	✓	✓
ReadyBoost	✓	✓	✓
Remote Media Streaming	✓	✓	✓
Sleep and Resume	✓	✓	✓
Snap	✓	✓	✓
Sticky Notes	✓	✓	✓
Supports 35 Languages			✓
System Restore	✓	✓	✓
Tablet PC	✓	✓	✓
User Account Control	✓	✓	✓
View Available Networks	✓	✓	✓
Windows Connect Now	✓	✓	✓
Windows Defender	✓	✓	✓
Windows Easy Transfer	✓	✓	✓
Windows Experience Index	✓	✓	✓
Windows Fax and Scan	✓	✓	✓
Windows Firewall	✓	✓	✓
Windows Media Center	✓	✓	✓
Windows Media Player 12	✓	✓	✓
Windows Search	✓	✓	✓
Windows Taskbar	✓	✓	✓
Windows Touch	✓	✓	✓
Windows Troubleshooting	✓	✓	✓
Windows Update	✓	✓	✓
Windows XP Mode		✓	✓
WordPad	✓	✓	✓
XPS	✓	✓	✓

Index

Note: **Boldfaced** page numbers refer to pages where key terms are defined.